To Keith
Merry Christmas
lots of love
Mike Richard and Paula
            xxx

The Third Time Around

The Third Time Around

The BOC Challenge 1990–91

Tony Fairchild

ROBERT HALE · LONDON

ISBN 0 7090 4550 6

Robert Hale Limited
Clerkenwell House
Clerkenwell Green
London EC1R 0HT

Photoset in Sabon in North Wales by
Derek Doyle & Associates, Mold, Clwyd.
Manufactured in Hong Kong
by Bookbuilders Ltd.

Contents

Illustrations

PICTURE CREDITS

John Rubython: 1, 3, 44–6, 64, 66, 69, 71, 87.
Barry Pickthall Picture Library: 2, 21–3, 25, 29–30, 33–4, 48–9, 51–4, 56–9, 61, 65, 68, 70, 73–9, 80–6, 88–93.
Roger Kennedy: 4, 27, 40.
Robert Hagan: 5, 7, 11, 18–19, 35, 47, 60, 62, 67.
Billy Black: 6, 8–10, 12–13, 15–17, 20, 24, 26, 28, 36–8, 41–3, 55.
Nandor Fa: 31–2, 72.
John Roberson: 39, 63.
Robin Davie: 50.
Map and diagram prepared by Eric W. Sponberg.

To all those who have, who do and who will continue to go down to the sea in tiny ships single-handed, and to my dear mother who passed away before she could read my account of this awesome adventure.

Overleaf   Accompanied by a fleet of spectator boats – The BOC Challengers crossed the start line at Newport, Rhode Island, at midday on 15 September 1990

Acknowledgements

The BOC racers of the 1990–91 who answered endless questions with great patience; Nigel Rowe who commissioned me to write the book; Lizzie Wilkinson, a tireless co-ordinator and collaborator and wonderful friend; Pete Dunning, whose Race Co-ordination included useful help on the book project; Barry Pickthall for the information so assiduously collected for *The Ultimate Challenge*, his account of the first BOC voyage, and *Around Alone* the official history of the second race which he wrote with Robin Knox-Johnston; Robin for providing me with a perfect foreword; Toni Dering and Ann Hughes for the endless useful tasks they performed so readily; and my wife Annie whose stoical long-suffering was as unflinching as ever.

T.F.

The BOC Group thanks IBM for their contribution to the event as Presenting Sponsor. The Group also acknowledges the support of other contributing sponsors including Champagne Mumm, AT&T, ICOM, and Magellan Systems.

THE COURSE OF THE BOC CHALLENGE

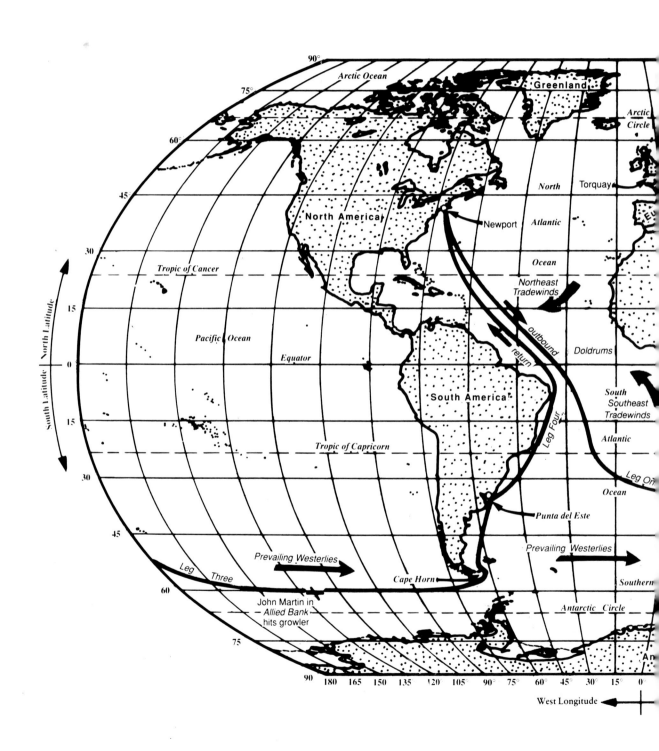

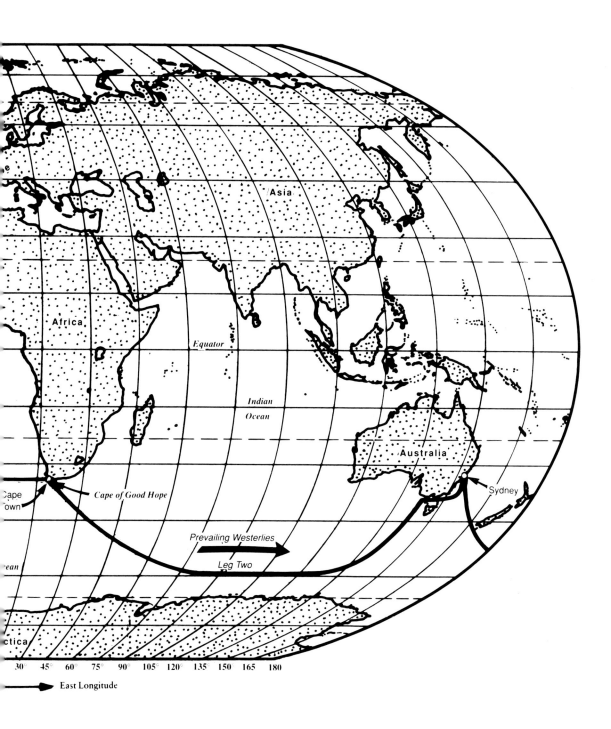

Asia

Africa

Equator

Indian
Ocean

Australia

Cape Town

Cape of Good Hope

Sydney

Prevailing Westerlies

Leg Two

ctica

30° 45° 60° 75° 90° 105° 120° 135° 150° 165° 180°

East Longitude

Right   Philippe Jeantot's *Credit Agricole IV* under way

Foreword

by Robin Knox-Johnston

It is not easy to decide when a sporting event becomes a classic, but it is now safe to say that The BOC Challenge has qualified. Since its inception in 1982, this longest of all the regular single-handed races has become acknowledged as the toughest individual contest open to men and women. The course, around the world, is the greatest possible sailing distance that can be devised, but distance alone does not make the Challenge a classic. The ultimate credit must go to the competitors who, with their dogged determination to compete through the harshest of environments, have produced so many shining examples of courage and seamanship that they are responsible for the Challenge's reputation and unique position in the world of sailing competition.

The origins of the Challenge lie with the development of single-handed racing after the Second World War. In 1960 five sailors set off on a race sponsored by the *Observer* newspaper from Plymouth to New York. The race became known as the OSTAR and has been run every four years. Encouraged by this success, longer voyages were made as the decade progressed, culminating with the *Sunday Times* Golden Globe Race in 1968 for the first non-stop single-handed circumnavigation. The Route du Rhum was France's answer to the OSTAR, and in America the Bermuda One Two and the Transpac created further regular single-handed events. After the 1976 OSTAR, a group of sailors meeting in one of the few locations where single-handers congregate – the Marina Pub on Goat Island in Newport, Rhode Island – discussed the ultimate single-handed race and concluded that it must be around the world.

One man, American David White, agreed to supervise the race organization. The competition was entitled 'Around Alone' and rules were published. These were not complicated since this was not perceived as an event requiring the policing of a normal offshore race, and it has always been axiomatic in single-handed sailing, where the competitors may not sight anyone between the start and the finish, that competitors trust each other. David wanted to enter the race as well, and undertook the twin tasks of building a boat and attempting to find both a personal and a race sponsor.

A number of sailors around the world heard of the race and entries were received from Britain, France and the United States, as well as Japan, New Zealand, Australia, South Africa and Czechoslovakia. But although some of the individual competitors managed to obtain financial support, as 1981 passed the overall race organization still lacked money. At this moment one of the British entrants, Richard Broadhead, approached The BOC Group in the UK for support. The company policy was not to sponsor individuals, but Nigel Rowe, Chief Executive of Corporate Communications, was looking for a stimulating event which could be imaginatively employed to link the company's world-wide activities, and the race fitted the bill. Negotiations were concluded remarkably quickly, and David White was free to concentrate on his own preparations. It was at this point that I was invited to become Chairman of the Race Committee. The race plans required few changes, but the name was altered to The BOC Challenge.

As the boats assembled in Newport during August 1982 (there were seventeen sailors from eight different countries), one point was immediately obvious. Sixteen of the boats were conventional yachts, built to the latest ideas from the racing circuit or well-tried cruiser designs. The exception was a French boat *Credit Agricole*, sailed by an ex-professional diver Philippe Jeantot. It was almost as if a jet fighter had joined a competition for piston-engined aircraft. *Credit Agricole*, in design, style and innovative ideas was definitely from a future generation.

Soon after the race commenced in August 1982 two competitors pulled out, and then two more, including David White, decided to call it a day in Cape Town. On the second leg from Cape Town to Sydney, *Lady Pepperell* lost her keel, and skipper Tony Lush had to be rescued by a fellow competitor, Francis Stokes. Sir Francis Chichester's last yacht *Gipsy Moth V*, sailed by Desmond Hampton, went ashore on Gabo Island off the Australian coast whilst her skipper was asleep. This accident was additionally unfortunate in that the boat had been the only one to supply serious opposition for Jeantot during the race. On the third leg, and in the empty wastes of the Southern Ocean south of the Pacific Ocean, Frenchman Jacques de Roux's yacht was dismasted and holed by the broken spars. For three days he bailed for his life, whilst Richard Broadhead struggled back against the wind and seas to effect an amazing rescue. After the boats rounded the infamous Cape Horn, everyone breathed a sigh of relief and headed for Rio de Janeiro, the last stop. At this stage, barring an accident, Philippe Jeantot had the race in the bag, and predictably this superb seaman was the first of the competitors to return to Newport in a new record time for a single-handed circumnavigation of just over 159 days, eleven days ahead of his nearest rival, Bertie Reed of South Africa.

Before the second Challenge could be organized, the committee had to examine the lessons learned from the first. The people who could best contribute were the contestants, and a meeting was held between the committee and all ten of the finishers to consider improvements for the future. The first decision was to allow the boats to be extended to sixty feet in length (the size then accepted world-wide as the maximum length for single-handed sailing). Jacques de Roux's ordeal of bailing for three days led to the introduction of new bulkhead requirements which ensured that if a boat were holed, it would remain buoyant and thus provide shelter for the sailor. The final rule concerned the introduction of water-ballast tanks to give greater stability and power to windward.

One of the successes of the race was the very stringent qualification requirement that each competitor must sail his/her boat across an ocean on a passage of at least 2,000 miles. This ensured that all contestants were familiar with their craft and were already seasoned single-handers before they were allowed to start. The first leg of nearly 8,000 miles down the Atlantic to Cape Town also serves as a final test, and nearly all the retirements from the races have occurred here as sailors contemplate their performance and realize that either their boats are unsuitable, or that they, as individuals, are not yet ready for the Southern Ocean.

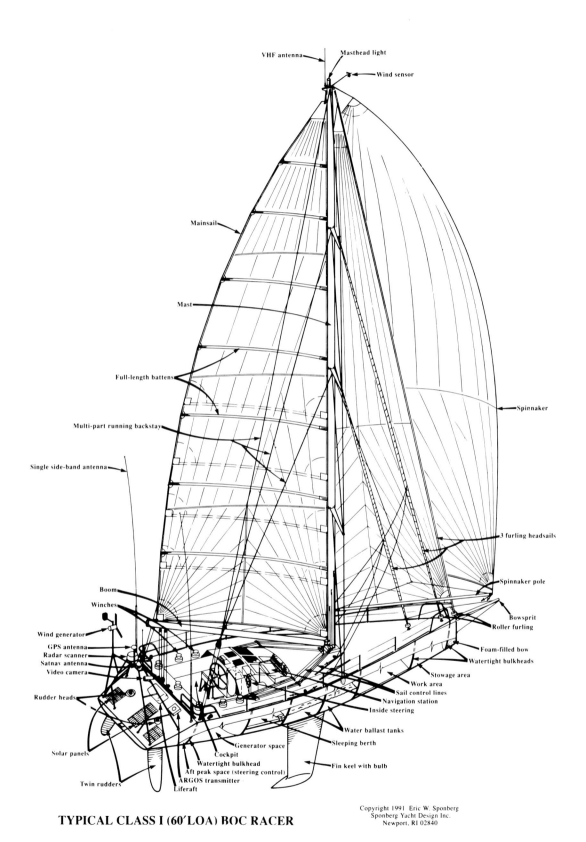

VHF antenna — Masthead light
Wind sensor

Mainsail

Mast

Full-length battens

Multi-part running backstay

Single side-band antenna

Spinnaker

3 furling headsails

Spinnaker pole

Boom

Winches

Bowsprit
Roller furling

Wind generator
GPS antenna
Radar scanner
Satnav antenna
Video camera

Foam-filled bow
Watertight bulkheads

Stowage area
Work area
Sail control lines
Navigation station
Inside steering

Rudder heads

Water ballast tanks
Sleeping berth

Solar panels

Generator space
Cockpit
Watertight bulkhead
Aft peak space (steering control)
ARGOS transmitter
Liferaft

Twin rudders

Fin keel with bulb

TYPICAL CLASS I (60′ LOA) BOC RACER

Copyright 1991 Eric W. Sponberg
Sponberg Yacht Design Inc.
Newport, RI 02840

THE THIRD TIME AROUND

As the entry forms for the second Challenge began to arrive at race headquarters, it was confirmed that this race would be far more serious than the first. A major change was the number of heavily sponsored entrants. As a result of this money, a new type of exciting short-handed long-distance racing-yacht had evolved from the original *Credit Agricole*. Freed from the constraints of restrictive handicap rules, and limited solely by length and stability, naval architects were able to break away from the existing racing mould and create boats designed for out-and-out speed, but combined with sufficient ruggedness to survive the Southern Ocean.

The larger boats, although superficially different in appearance, had a number of important similarities. Plumb bows, to give the maximum water-line length, were chosen by nearly everyone, and, despite the claim that this would lead boats to nose-dive when running fast in a following sea, the sailors found in practice that they suffered no more than conventional boats when hard-pressed. Twin rudders were installed on most boats so that whatever angle of heel the boat reached, there was always one rudder almost vertical to give maximum steering control. All the boats had fully battened mainsails, which not only enabled them to set a greater sail area, but also to cut down wear and tear on the sails. Cockpits were simple, usually with a small shelter at the forward end and with open sterns to drain water quickly. Ballast tanks, some of which were filled by sea-water pressure created by the boat's movement, were common. A few boats continued to carry the windvane self-steering equipment, but the majority now depended upon electronic systems which responded very promptly to the sudden yaws that are run-of-the-mill when sailing in huge seas.

The BOC boat, as the new type was christened, was a quantum leap into the future as far as monohulls were concerned; light and strong, with the looks and speed of a thoroughbred racehorse.

Improvements to boat performance had necessarily to be matched by innovation in control. Navigation equipment moved into the computer age, and in certain cases the onboard facilities were linked directly with machines ashore. However, if such developments tended to create technicians amongst the contestants, there was to be no substitute for skill and hard work when trying to coax the maximum speed from a boat in the Doldrums or handling a recalcitrant spinnaker in the Southern Ocean when a front came through and suddenly increased the wind from Force 2 to Force 10.

The twenty-five strong fleet sailed from Newport in August 1986, but the second BOC Challenge was not destined to be a simple repeat of the first. Boats retired from quite early on in the race, one through a collision with a submerged object, others because of damage or as tired and exhausted sailors made decisions they would regret for the rest of their lives. The new sixty-footers produced much closer racing, and a battle royal ensued at the front of the fleet.

Tragically, Jacques de Roux, who had entered again in a very fast 50-footer in which he had an unbeatable lead in Class II, disappeared from his boat as it closed Sydney. This affected deeply all who had known this quiet, friendly, but exceedingly tough man. Another Class II boat was dismasted shortly after passing New Zealand, but Canadian John Hughes pluckily sailed on around Cape Horn under jury rig to the Falkland Islands where a new mast could be stepped. Jeantot won again, and reduced his time to just over 134 days, but he did not have it all his own way, and could only win one of the legs. His average performance, however, gave him overall victory, although the second boat, sailed by fellow Frenchman Titouan Lamazou, was only three days behind.

FOREWORD

An amazing improvement of nearly twenty per cent in the performance between the first and second Challenges indicated just how much the boats had progressed as a result of the races. Their performance was equivalent to conventional racing-boats more than a third longer. Such an enormous advance is a result of revolution rather than evolution in design and, unless there is to be a major change in the boat lengths allowed, it is difficult to foresee how there can ever be such a large jump again.

The story of the third Challenge is not just another rerun of the first two, it is the next instalment in an unfolding saga. The course was slightly different and, although there were familiar faces amongst the contestants, there were also many new ones. There was a trend among the latest BOC boats to be wider than their predecessors, and with ballast tanks they tended to be even more powerful to windward. New boats and equipment were tested, and the lessons learned will filter through to the boating industry eventually and again boost the quality of the world's yachting fleets. The weather conditions will always vary in this Everest of yacht races, making the third Challenge a continuing tale of individual determination and triumph over adversity.

The BOC Challenge is established as the major international single-handed competition. Perhaps even more, the Challenge has produced the toughest voluntary test yet devised for individuals – anyone who completes the arduous course is a winner.

Overleaf Crowds packed the Newport waterfront on 15 September
1990, the day the race began

27

The BOC Challenge
1990–91 Entrants

David Adams
Innkeeper

Rig; Sloop
Specs.: LOA 60'0'' (18.3 m). Beam 14'7''
(4.5 m). Draft 9'9'' (3.0 m). Disp.
24,250 lb (11,000 kg)
Designer: Kell Steinman
Sponsor: Yalumba Angas Brut (wine),
MMI (insurance), Cool Carriers (shipping)
and Country Road (menswear stores)

Born: 16 Dec. 1953　　　　**AUSTRALIA**

David Adams had a borrowed boat and a budget of
£45,000. Emulating his grandfather, a Cape Horn
clipper-ship sailor, Adams took up sailing at the age of
twelve. A master mariner, he left the Australian
merchant navy after thirteen years to prepare himself for
The BOC Challenge before which he had logged over
70,000 ocean miles delivering yachts and competing in
short-handed ocean races such as the two-handed
Melbourne–Osaka race in 1987. His yacht for The BOC
Challenge was a successful two-year-old 60-foot
aluminium ULDB with a fractional sloop rig and
modified deck layout and sail-handling systems for
single-handing.

Christophe Auguin
Groupe Sceta

Born: 10 Dec. 1959

FRANCE

Christophe Auguin's career has moved from RORC and Formula 40 events to single-handed ocean racing. He competed in five Figaro races, winning the single-handed prize in 1986. He founded Mer et Communications, a sports marketing company. Auguin commissioned the design team of Groupe Finot to draft a third-generation 60-footer BOC racer that was among the beamiest in the fleet. The composite hull was built by the Mark Pinta yard in La Rochelle. The yacht had an 89-foot carbon-fibre mast with two sail plan options.

Rig: Sloop
Specs.: LOA 60'0'' (18.3 m). Beam 19'0'' (5.8 m). Draft 12'0'' (3.7 m). Disp. 25,000 lb (11.340 kg)
Designer: Groupe Finot
Sponsor: Groupe Sceta (commercial transportation and tourism)

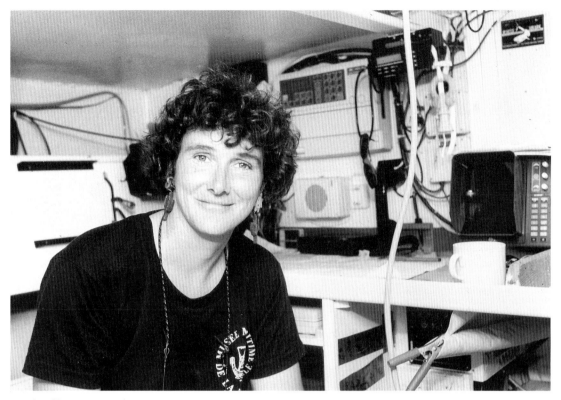

Isabelle Autissier
Ecureuil Poitou-Charentes
(ex-36.15 Met)

Born: 18 Oct. 1956

FRANCE

Rig: Cutter
Specs.: LOA 60'0'' (18.3 m). Beam 11'3'' (3.4 m). Draft 9'8'' (2.9 m). Disp. 20,500 lb (9,300 kg)
Designer: Philippe Harle/Alain Mortain
Sponsor: Couisses d'Epargne Ecureuil de Poitou-Charentes (bank), Secretariat d'états charge du droit des femmes, and Conseil Regional de Poitou-Charentes

Isabelle Autissier, an engineer and marine science professor from La Rochelle, has sailed since the age of seven. She took up single-handed racing 'for self-improvement' three years before her BOC entry and has competed in a Mini-Transat and two Figaro races. In May 1990 she purchased the knifelike, aluminium 60-footer that Jean-Luc van den Heede sailed to third place in the first, 1989, Globe Challenge. She modified the rig for better light-air performance and enclosed a portion of the cockpit for shelter, but the boat was still the narrowest and among the most spartan of the fleet.

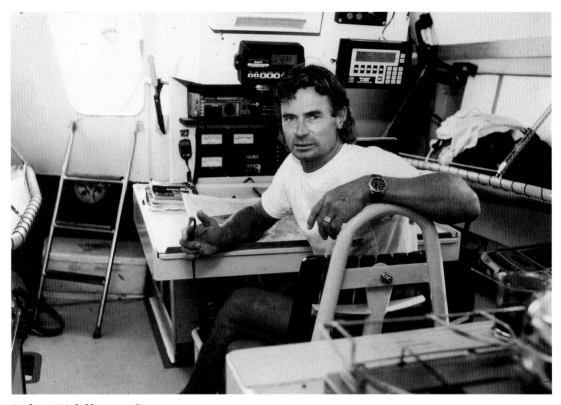

John Biddlecombe
Interox Crusader
(ex-*ACI Crusader*)

Born: 23 Apr. 1944   **AUSTRALIA**

Rig: Cutter
Specs.: LOA 60'0'' (18.3 m). Beam 14'3''
(4.3 m). Draft 12'3'' (3.7 m). Disp.
26,000 lb (11,794 kg)
Designer: Paul Lucas
Sponsor: Interox Chemicals

Sydney boatbuilder and designer John Biddlecombe entered the 1986 BOC Challenge, but was forced to retire when, just sixty-two miles short of the Leg 1 finish line, the boat began taking on water and he accepted a tow into Cape Town. He entered the third BOC with the same French-built and designed 60-foot *Crusader* and was confident he had solved her earlier stability problems for the 1990 race. Biddlecombe sold his boatbuilding company to focus his efforts on the race.

Kanga Birtles
Jarkan Yacht Builders

Rig: Sloop
Specs.: LOA 60′00″ (18.3 m). Beam 15′6″ (4.7 m). Draft 10′2″ (3.1 m). Disp. 25,760 lb (11,685 kg)
Designer: John King
Sponsor: Jarkan Yacht Builders

Born: 25 Feb. 1943   **AUSTRALIA**

For Richard (Kanga) Birtles, The BOC Challenge was 'the culmination of a lifetime of dedication to sailing.' He cut his teeth racing dinghies on Sydney Harbour. With 100,000 miles of ocean voyaging to his credit, including nine Sydney-Hobart classics, seamanship and organization are his strengths. His boat was a powerful 60-foot sloop designed by John King expressly for the race and constructed by Birtles' own boatbuilding firm of Jarkan Pty. Ltd., which has built some 250 yachts since 1975.

Nandor Fa
Alba Regia

Rig: Sloop
Specs.: LOA 60'0'' (18.3 m). Beam 16'0'' (4.9 m). Draft: 10'6'' (3.2 m). Disp. 20,943 lb (9,500 kg)
Designer: Nandor Fa
Sponsor: Alba Regia (construction), Kofem, Malev (Hungarian airline), Trading and Credit Bank of Hungary, Helia-D (cosmetics)

HUNGARY   **Born**: 9 July 1953

Nandor Fa's path from landlocked Hungary to the starting line off Newport is one of the most intriguing East–West sagas in BOC history. He took up sailing at twenty-seven, and three years later was crowned Hungarian Finn champion. When his Olympic hopes were dashed by the 1984 Soviet boycott, he and a friend scraped together funds for a small boat and circled the globe. With partial backing from five Hungarian companies and help from friends, he built his Airex-cored fibreglass sloop on a shoestring budget, hoping to finish in the top ten.

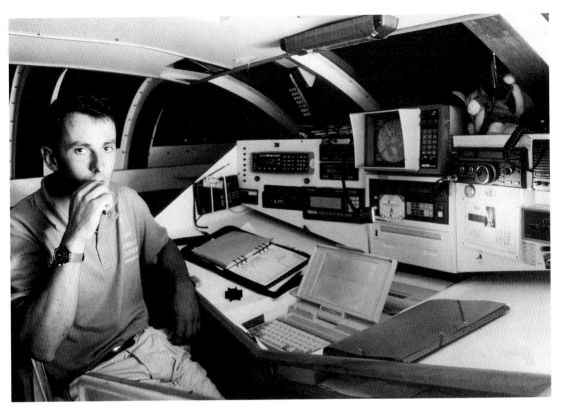

Alain Gautier
Generali Concorde

Born: 8 May 1962

FRANCE

Rig: Sloop
Specs.: LOA 60'0" (18.3 m). Beam 19'0" (5.8 m). Draft 12'6" (3.8 m). Disp. 26,000 lb (11,793 kg)
Designer: Jean-Marie Finot, Pascal Conq
Sponsor: Generali Concorde (Franco-Italian insurance group)

When asked how long he has been sailing, 28-year-old Alain Gautier quips that he was conceived on board his parents' cruising yacht in the Gulf of Morbihan. He stepped into the solo sailing limelight in 1989 when he won the Figaro race that year. His victory secured him a generous sponsorship package from Generali Concorde and a stunning new aluminium Finot/Conq design that he sailed to a sixth-place finish in the Globe Challenge. Despite rigging problems and some difficulty in managing his beamy boat in the Southern Ocean, his remarkable 133-day passage at the age of twenty-seven earned him a place in the record books as the youngest man to circle the world alone without stopping.

Philippe Jeantot
Credit Agricole IV

Born: 8 May 1952   **FRANCE**

The influence on single-handed yacht racing of Philippe Jeantot may be as significant as that of The BOC Challenge, the race he won in both 1982–83 and 1986–87. A professional hard-hat diver turned race-boat driver, Jeantot was virtually unknown when he arrived at the start of the first race in 1982 with a radical, water-ballasted 56-footer from designer Guy Ribadeau-Dumas. When he led every leg of the race and won handily in 159 days, his route became the textbook course and *Credit Agricole* the paradigm BOC boat that has influenced second- and third-generation BOC designs. In 1986–87 he set a new course record of 134 days, a benchmark he hoped to better with the new composite boat that he sailed alone non-stop around the world in the Globe Challenge, which he founded.

Rig: Sloop
Specs.: LOA 60′0″ (18.3 m). Beam 18′3″ (5.6 m). Draft 12′7″ (3.8 m). Disp. 25,353 lb (11,500 kg)
Designer: Marc Lombard
Sponsor: Credit Agricole (bank)

John Martin
Allied Bank

Rig: Sloop
Specs.: LOA 60'0'' (18.3 m). Beam 19'7''
(6.0 m). Draft 13'1'' (4.0 m). Disp.
23,529 lb (10,672 kg)
Designer: Angelo Lavranos
Sponsor: Allied Bank

Born: 8 Oct. 1954　　　　　　　　**SOUTH AFRICA**

Lifelong sailor John Martin won the first and last legs of the 1986 BOC Challenge, setting records for each of them; but was dogged by a severe shortage of funds and a broken auto-pilot, resulting in a fifth-place standing in Class I. He entered the third BOC with a generous sponsorship package and a radical third-generation speedster. *Allied Bank* was the beamiest and among the lightest in Class I with a hull of prepregnated carbon-fibre and Kevlar, and a powerful 80-foot carbon-fibre rig. The Atomic Energy Commission helped to develop the low-drag dagger keel and supplied irradiated food for the voyage.

Enda O'Coineen
Kilcullen
(ex-*Thursday's Child*)

Rig: Sloop
Specs.: LOA 60'00'' (18.3 m). Beam, 14'7'' (4.5 m). Draft 11'5'' (3.5 m). Disp. 18,500 lb (8,400 kg)
Designer: Lindenberg/Bergstrom
Sponsor: Smirnoff (spirits)

IRELAND   **Born**: 15 Oct. 1955

Enda O'Coineen of Dun Laoghaire, Ireland, had hoped to build a Class I boat for The BOC Challenge, but instead chartered Warren Luhrs' former *Thursday's Child*, which in 1989 smashed *Flying Cloud*'s New York-to-San Francisco record. She was specifically built for The BOC Challenge 1986–87. According to her skipper, *Kilcullen* is the name of an ancient Irish kingdom in the West Indies. A journalist and publisher, he is also an experienced ocean-racing yachtsman and entrepreneur. In 1985 he secured his place in the annals of strange voyages in unlikely craft when he made a 28-day solo Atlantic crossing in a 16-foot inflatable propelled by a 55 h.p. outboard and a small sail.

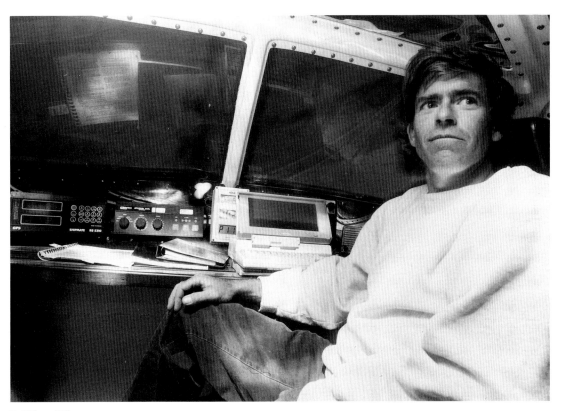

Mike Plant
Duracell

Born: 21 Nov. 1950   **UNITED STATES**

Rig: Sloop
Specs.: LOA 60′0″ (18.3 m). Beam 15′0″ (4.6 m). Draft 11′6″ (3.5 m). Disp., 27,500 lb (12,474 kg)
Designer: Rodger Martin
Sponsor: Duracell (batteries)

Mike Plant knows the rigours of the Southern Ocean and has tasted victory and defeat on two notable solo circumnavigations. In the 1986–87 BOC Challenge he won Class II in *Airco Distributor*, a Rodger Martin-designed 50-footer that he built. Next, Plant commissioned Martin to design a 60-footer that could compete in both the Globe Challenge and The BOC Challenge 1990–91. Mike's hopes for victory in the Globe were dashed when a rigging problem forced him into Campbell Island, south of New Zealand, but he finished the circumnavigation in 134 days and set a new American record (with one stop).

Bertie Reed
Grinaker

Rig: Sloop
Specs.: LOA 60′0″ (18.3 m). Beam 15′0″ (4.6 m). Draft 11′3″ (3.4 m). Disp. 27,000 lb (12,247 kg)
Designer: Rodger Martin
Sponsor: Grinaker (electronics)

SOUTH AFRICA   **Born**: 19 Jan. 1945

Back for his third run in The BOC Challenge was 'Biltong' Bertie Reed, South Africa's best-known yachtsman. As a career naval warrant officer, Reed had the enviable job of teaching sailing and campaigning boats in the OSTAR, Round Britain, Cape Town to Rio race, and the 1982–83 BOC Challenge, where he pushed the aged *Voortrekker* (built 1968) to a remarkable second-place finish. After leaving the navy, he completed the 1986–87 BOC in a modified IOR racer, then, with major sponsorship from an electronics firm, commissioned Martin to design *Grinaker* which is built of a combination of Kevlar, carbon-fibre and fibreglass skins on a PVC foam core. Rudder and auto-pilot problems thwarted his chances to complete the Globe Challenge.

Jose de Ugarte
BBV Expo '92
(ex-*Lada Poch III*)

Rig: Sloop
Specs.: LOA 60'0'' (18.3 m). Beam 15'4''
(4.7 m). Draft 11'8'' (3.6 m). Disp.
26,455 lb (12,000 kg)
Designer: Bouvet/Petit
Sponsor: Banco Bilbao Vizcaya (bank)

Born: 6 Nov. 1928   **SPAIN**

At sixty-two, Spain's premier single-handed sailor has no plans to grow old gracefully. *BBV Expo '92* has made two solo circumnavigations in the last four years, placing second in both the 1986–87 BOC Challenge and in the 1989 Globe Challenge (when the yacht was named *Lada Poch III*. The lifelong sailor and master mariner's first yacht was a husky 45-foot fishing-smack that he sailed single-handed between Ireland and Spain. He has completed three OSTARs, and in the 1988 event was the third monohull to finish, squeezing out even his current boat, then named *Ecureuil d'Aquitaine* and skippered by Titouan Lamazou. He is backed by the biggest bank in Spain.

Jack Boye
Project City Kids
(ex-*Tuesday's Child*)

Rig: Sloop
Specs.: LOA 49'11'' (15.2 m). Beam 11'4'' (3.5 m). Draft 9'0'' (2.7 m). Disp. 18,500 lb (8,392 kg)
Designer: John Cherubini
Unsponsored

UNITED STATES   **Born**: 2 Oct. 1943

Jack Boye, a retired stockbroker from New York, spent his boyhood sailing class boats and one-design racers on New Jersey's coastal bays. He earned a football scholarship at Penn State University and was a highly decorated Army captain in Vietnam. He sold his own investment firm, Legend Securities, to pursue other interests such as The BOC Challenge. *Project City Kids* was a highly modified and shortened Hunter 54 originally built for Warren Luhrs' ill-fated 1980 OSTAR campaign. Boye has raced her hard the last eight years, successfully completing four Bermuda One-Two Races, two single-handed transatlantic races and the galeswept 1986 Route du Rhum.

Yves Dupasquier
Servant IV

Rig: Sloop
Specs.: LOA 50'0'' (15.2 m). Beam 13'1''
(4.0 m). Draft 8'7'' (2.6 m). Disp.
12,125 lb (5,500 kg)
Designer: Jean Beret
Sponsor: Servant Software

Born: 24 Mar. 1961   **FRANCE**

Yves Dupasquier has made a dozen transatlantic passages including winning his class in the 1984 Quebec–San Malo classic and competing two Mini-Transats. A skilled boat builder, he was part of the team that built *Ecureuil d'Aquitaine* for Lamazou's 1986 BOC effort. While seeking sponsorship for his own 1990 bid, Dupasquier and four boatbuilding, hang-gliding friends obtained a bank loan and in six months built the ultralight flyer they named for their favourite hang-gliding stunt, the loop-the-loop. *Looping* turned in impressive daily runs on her qualifier and, true to her name, weathered two rollovers. For the race she was renamed *Servant IV*.

Josh Hall
New Spirit of Ipswich
(ex-*Airco Distributor*)

Rig: Sloop
Specs.: LOA 50'0'' (15.2 m). Beam 13'9''
(4.2 m). Draft 9'0'' (2.7 m). Disp.
24,000 lb (10,886 kg)
Designer: Rodger Martin
Sponsor: 30 companies

GREAT BRITAIN   **Born**: 18 May 1962

For likeable Josh Hall, competing in the BOC marks
both the pinnacle of his professional sailing career and
an opportunity for community involvement. Some thirty
Ipswich businesses contributed to his grassroots
campaign. From a childhood of dinghy sailing, Josh's
big break came at the age of twenty when he helped to
build the catamaran *British Airways* and spent the next
three years sailing with Robin Knox-Johnston. He was
placed fifth in his class in the 1988 Single-handed
Transatlantic Race and later that year bought 1986
BOC Class II winner *Airco Distributor* in which he
sailed alone across the Atlantic and his monohull class
in the 1989 Round Britain Race.

The new, solid silver BOC Challenge perpetual trophy,
designed by Garrard's of London

Christophe Auguin's *Groupe Sceta* – a typical example of the archetypal 'BOC boat'

Jarkan Yacht Builders and (*below*) *Innkeeper*. Kanga Birtles and David Adams had a race within a race to be top Australian

Right   John Martin's *Allied Bank* with a beam of six metres was the beamiest boat in the race. A collision with a 'growler' in the Southern Ocean put paid to his excellent chances of winning

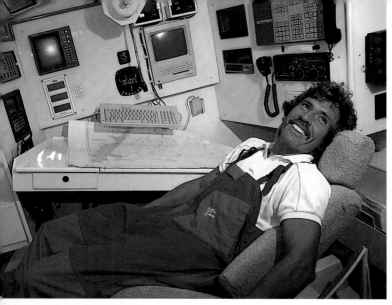

Philippe Jeantot at *Credit Agricole*'s highly sophisticated nav station. His seat and chart table are gimballed so that they remain level regardless of the heel of the boat

Right   Philippe Jeantot was aiming for his third BOC Challenge victory in his new *Credit Agricole IV*

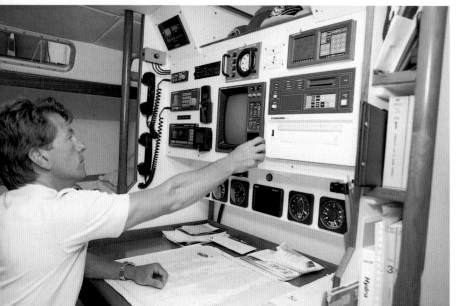

Corinthian Robert Hooke at the nav station of *Niihau 4*

Jack Boye's *Project City Kids*: one of the more spartan interiors of the fleet

Iceberg and Southern Ocean waves by Nandor Fa. The ice hazards of the Southern Ocean meant long watches and little sleep for all the competitors

Left *Alba Regia*: built on a shoestring budget by her skipper Nandor Fa

Jane Weber's *Tilley Endurable*. Her BOC Challenge ended prematurely on the first leg to Cape Town

Minoru Saito's *Shutendohji II* was built by fellow skipper Don McIntyre

Don McIntyre
Buttercup
(ex-*Sponsor Wanted*)

Rig: Sloop
Specs.: LOA 49'11'' (15.2 m). Beam 12'0''
(3.7 m). Draft 9'6'' (2.9 m). Disp.
17,500 lb (7,938 kg)
Designer: Joe Adams/Graham Radford
Sponsor: Buttercup Bakeries, Goodman
Fielder Wattie

Born: 5 Jan. 1955   **AUSTRALIA**

Don McIntyre, a boatbuilder from Spit Junction, New South Wales, began sailing dinghies at the age of ten and at twenty-three embarked on a three-year, 14,000-mile Pacific cruise in a homebuilt 29-footer. He is the founder of the Shorthanded Sailing Association of Australia and organizer of the Around Australia Race. Insufficient funds prevented him from competing in the 1986–87 BOC Challenge, so when his 50-footer aluminium sloop was launched last April, he unabashedly christened her *Sponsor Wanted* and painted his phone number on the hull in an attempt to attract financial support. He did so in Sydney at the half-way stage. He built both his own boat and a 50-footer for fellow competitor Minoru Saito of Japan.

UNITED STATES   **Born:** 15 Jan. 1927

Hal Roth
Sebago
(ex-*American Flag*)

Rig: Cutter
Specs.: LOA 49'9'' (15.2 m). Beam 12'0''
(3.7 m). Draft 8'0'' (2.4 m). Disp.
19,000 lb (8,618 kg)
Designer: Bill Lee
Sponsor: Sebago (shoes)

Back for his second run in The BOC Challenge was
63-year-old author Hal Roth. He not only competed in
the 1986 race; he chronicled the saga of the twenty-five
who entered in his seventh book, *Chasing the Long
Rainbow*. Roth was a full-keel man who in twenty-five
years of cruising with his wife Margaret had logged
150,000 miles before entering the 1986 BOC Challenge
with the light-displacement Santa Cruz 50, *American
Flag*. Without sponsorship, he completed the course in
171 days, placing fourth in Class II. With backing from
Sebago, Roth lightened the boat and added water-
ballast tanks and a lighter, taller rig to take part in the
1990–91 BOC Challenge.

Yukoh Tada
Koden VIII

Born: 10 April 1930

JAPAN

Rig: Cutter
Specs.: LOA 50'0'' (15.2 m). Beam 13'7'' (4.1 m). Draft 6'6'' (2.0 m). Disp. 11,023 lb (5,000 kg)
Designer: Yukoh Tada
Sponsor: Koden Electronics

In the gallery of single-handed sailors, there was only one Yukoh Tada – Tokyo taxi-driver, abstract artist, amateur jazz musician, Zen Buddhist and one of the most likeable eccentrics in the sport. Tada took up sailing twenty-five years ago and completed a number of Pacific single-handed races before winning Class II of the 1982–83 BOC Challenge. In 1987, he was sixth in the double-handed Melbourne–Osaka race. He was later able to add 'yacht designer' to his long list of accomplishments by drafting his own innovative boat for The BOC Challenge 1990–91. At 11,000 pounds, *Koden VIII* was the lightest in the fleet, but Tada found room for a sophisticated array of electronics, his tenor sax, electronic organ, paintbrushes and easel.

Jane Weber
Tilley Endurable

Rig: Cutter
Specs.: LOA 42'0'' (12.8 m). Beam 13'2'' (4.0 m). Draft 5'7'' (1.7 m). Disp. 22,000 lb (9,980 kg)
Designer: German Frers
Sponsor: Tilley Endurables (outdoor clothing)

CANADA   **Born**: 12 May 1945

Jane Weber, a 45-year-old grandmother of three, was the first woman to enter The BOC Challenge 1990–91. At the age of twelve she emigrated with her family from Bristol, England, to Canada, but it was not until the break-up of her marriage in 1982 that she set out in search of adventure. On a series of eight cruising boats, she worked her way to Florida, the Caribbean and across the Pacific, covering some 28,000 miles in twenty-six months. Back in Toronto, she financed her modified Beneteau 42 by working as a real estate agent before selling her home and throwing her Tilley hat into The BOC Challenge 1990–91.

Robin Davie
Global Exposure

Rig: Cutter
Specs.: LOA 40'0'' (12.2 m). Beam 11'8''
(3.6 m). Draft 7'0'' (2.1 m). Disp.
17,920 lb (8,130 kg)
Designer: Bergstrom/Ridder
Unsponsored

Born: 2 Nov. 1951   **GREAT BRITAIN**

Robin Davie, a British merchant navy officer from Cornwall, first went to sea on the three-masted training ship *Sir Winston Churchill* as a sixteenth-birthday gift, and ten years ago set his sights on The BOC Challenge. For the first race he built his own ferrocement 40-footer, but his solo qualifying run to Cape Town convinced him that he needed more experience and money. Next, with *Global Exposure*, he qualified for the 1986 race, and tried every fundraising scheme from running a 336-mile marathon to soliciting 800 corporations, but came up short. He has since refitted the boat and completed the 1988 single-handed Transatlantic. His seventeen-year-old boat was the smallest and oldest in the fleet.

William Gilmore
Zafu

Rig: Sloop
Specs.: LOA 44'5'' (13.5 m). Beam 13'7''
(4.1 m). Draft 8'0'' (2.4 m). Disp.
20,600 lb (9.344 kg)
Designer: Rodney Johnstone
Unsponsored

UNITED STATES   **Born**: 20 Nov. 1936

Bill Gilmore is at heart a cruising sailor who describes
his sailing experience as a lifelong infection with
intermittent remissions. He is known for a ready wit
that belies considerable experience with more than
30,000 blue water miles. After operating a party fishing
business in Florida, he built a traditional three-masted
schooner and moved his family to New England. He
entered the 1988 single-handed Transatlantic Race with
a J/37, but was forced into the Azores for repairs. For
the third BOC Challenge he chose a J/44 – a standard
GRP boat with some modifications.

Robert Hooke
Niihau 4

Rig: Cutter
Specs.: LOA 44'3'' (13.5 m). Beam 14'1''
(4.3 m). Draft 7'6'' (2.3 m). Disp.
20,000 lb (9,072 kg).
Designer: Ron Holland
Unsponsored

Born: 12 Sept. 1942   **UNITED STATES**

London-based Robert Hooke is a native of New Jersey.
He served as a naval officer in the Pacific and in
Vietnam, before moving twelve years ago to London
where he manages the equities department of the French
Banque Paribas. He has owned four boats, all named
Niihau after an isolated Hawaiian island, and has made
a 5,000-mile transatlantic voyage and was placed fourth
in class in the 1989 Round Britain Race. *Niihau 4* was a
customized racing version of the Holland-designed,
Kirie-built *Feeling* 13.50 with a deep keel, stripped-out
interior, water ballast and rigid dodger.

Minoru Saito
Shutendohji II

Rig: Cutter
Specs.: LOA 50′0′′ (15.2 m). Beam 12′0′′
(3.7 m). Draft 4′1′′ (12.2 m). Disp.
19,000 lb (8,618 kg)
Designer: Adams/Radford
Unsponsored

JAPAN   **Born**: 7 Jan. 1934

While Minoru Saito of Japan is a relative newcomer to
the short-handed racing scene, he compressed a lot of
blue water miles into three years of single-handed racing
in preparation for The BOC Challenge. The 56-year-old
Tokyo native's first major single-handed contest was the
1987 Melbourne-Osaka Race. When major compli-
cations forced him to retire to Sydney, he then competed
in the double-handed Sydney–Yokosuka Race later that
year. In 1988 he completed the single-handed Japan–
Sydney Race and, before a heart attack forced his
withdrawal, was an entrant in the Round Australia
Race. In 1989 he finished third in the Auckland–
Fukuoka Race. For The BOC Challenge, he commissioned fellow race entrant Don McIntyre of Australia to
build a 50-foot cutter that was similar to McIntyre's
own entry.

Paul Thackaberry
Volcano

Rig: Cutter
Specs.: LOA 49'11'' (15.2 m). Beam 11'6''
(3.5 m). Draft 8'0'' (2.4 m). Disp.
16,000 lb (7,258 kg)
Designer: Paul Thackaberry
Unsponsored

Born: 28 June 1952   **UNITED STATES**

Paul Thackaberry, a 38-year-old tool-and-die-maker
from Oxford, Michigan, has come a long way since
taking up sailing in 1973. 'I bought my first boat for
$3,000 and immediately sank her,' he says. 'So I got a
library book and taught myself to sail.' He has since
logged 20,000 solo miles between the Great Lakes and
the Caribbean. He was a provisional entry in the last
BOC Challenge, and worked for five years to design and
build his own boat for the third. *Volcano* (named after a
Jimmy Buffet song) resembles a scaled-up International
14 with a flat bottom, tandem keel terminating in a
torpedo bulb and twin rudders. The hull was
constructed of epoxy and fibreglass over strip-planked
cedar, and Thackaberry made much of the hardware
himself.

Right   Alain Gautier's *Generali Concorde* was first across the line in
Cape Town, but his 16½ hour time penalty for his late arrival
in Newport relegated him to fourth place

1　A Cast of Twenty-Five

The final blow came on 3 December 1990, deep into the Southern Ocean, eight days out of Cape Town.

The port rudder disappeared. It couldn't have been the force of the water. The fitting was too sturdy. It had to have been a collision with a whale. The disaster shattered all the hopes Nandor Fa had invested in the 60-foot *Alba Regia* he had designed and built himself. He could not steer the boat downwind. He would not conquer the world this trip. In the huge, confused seas kicked up by 50-knot winds, he would have to return whence he came for repairs. The rudder was lost the day after the one on the starboard side broke. It was the latest and worst luck in a succession of misfortunes, and after some 12,000 sea miles it was a mighty blow.

Back in August, when Nandor began the voyage from Gibraltar, he had gone to sea desperately sick. No one knew what was wrong with him. He had been given medicine and some guidance. He had ignored advice not to sail; to meet deadlines and, above all, to satisfy an unfathomable desire to race around the world alone. He had been seriously ill for several days, but he pulled through. He soldiered on for Cape Town after a minor collision, after equipment failure, and despite steering problems resulting from the broken starboard rudder stock; the one that was to fail first in the Southern Ocean. The Southern Ocean failure was very different. That was to spell the end of Nandor's hopes of finishing near the front of the fleet at the end of the race. In a very important way that, for him, was the end.

Nandor Fa was born 9 July 1953, one of four brothers in Szekesfehervar, a small town some sixty kilometres from Budapest. He came late to sailing. First he had shown promise as a wrestler, a sport he had to quit when he was just seventeen because of a knee injury. For another ten years he was a canoeist. He didn't win any prizes. 'The prizes', he says, 'were the lessons of life; it made me human.'

It was when he was twenty-seven that he switched to the sport of Finn dinghy sailing. Within three years he had become the top ranked Finn dinghy sailor in his native Hungary. Finn sailors have to be athletes. Nandor Fa is an exceptional athlete. For fun when he was building *Alba Regia*, he took up Laser dinghy sailing. He became runner-up in his national Laser championship.

In his Finn dinghy days he had his sights firmly set on the Olympic Games in Los Angeles in 1984. He was selected as his country's representative. The boycott by the Iron Curtain countries put paid to that ambition.

He decided on another target: a circumnavigation. He built a boat and set sail with a friend. They began their two-handed circumnavigation from Gibraltar and completed their 717-day voyage via Cape Town, Sydney, Cape Horn, Rio de Janeiro and Gibraltar. The whole of Hungary followed their adventure. They became national heroes. The boat, the *Saint Jupat*, a Swedish designed fin-keel sloop, was exhibited at the Budapest Trade Fair. Nandor wrote a best-seller after the voyage that expressed his views on religion, friendship, work and communism.

During the voyage, Nandor stopped off to learn yacht design from Ben Lexcen; the man who drew the radical lines of the America's Cup-winning 12-metre yacht *Australia II*. And it was during his circumnavigation that he decided to build another boat; a 60-foot racing yacht. He wanted to take part in The BOC Challenge 1990–91, the four-stage, 27,000-mile round-the-world race for single-handers. That's sailing solo; unaided.

Nandor Fa's BOC dream had begun when he intercepted radio conversations between BOC competitors off Cape Horn when he was doing his two-handed circumnavigation.

Ben Lexcen gave Nandor the lines of a 60-footer. Nandor thought it was 'too conventional' and spent hours modifying the plans. He called his boat *Alba Regia*, the Latin name of his home-town, which gave him the most assistance, both financially and morally. He was their Sportsman of the Year in 1990.

He estimates that the boat cost him about £120,000. His sponsors were his home town of Szekesfehervar, once the capital of Hungary; Kofem, the most important aluminium company in Hungary in his home town; the Kereskedelmi Bank RT, the Commercial Bank Corporation of Hungary; Malev, the Hungarian national airline; Helia D, one of the favourite cosmetic companies in Hungary, and the Alba Regia building company in Szekesfehervar.

Around six foot, with blond hair cut only a millimetre short of a full 'Yul Brynner', Nandor has the physique of a middleweight wrestler. He went to Scandinavia for his mast, to Australia for his sails, to Czechoslovakia for fibreglass, and to Germany for carbon-fibre and fittings.

It was on the compulsory, 2,000-mile qualifying voyage for the BOC that he was ill. He couldn't delay his departure from Gibraltar for fear he would suffer a penalty for being late in Newport.

'Then I suffered the collision at the start. There are a lot of apologies, but my boat let through the water. I had to make repairs with adhesive tape; it's not the best thing. The boat is very fast, and could sail much faster. But I have to take care of her because of the only one set of sails and some damaged fittings.

'My Genoa is broken; I'm always sewing it. But this race is a good lesson for me. I thought it's enough to build a good, light boat and to have great enthusiasm. Now I see, it's not true. The chance depends on money. You mustn't save money on good fittings. But my budget is limited. And now I know, it would be useful to spend about £120,000 for my boat. She could be competitive. So I have to sail for safety.'

He was just as stoical about the broken rudders in the Southern Ocean. He said: 'I repaired the first one and it didn't take too long. It just meant I would be a bit slower to

Sydney. I was not too dismayed. Then, early on 3 December, I lost completely the other rudder.

'I could not steer the boat. At first I went slowly to the south. I need some hours to turn back. I could not reach or run. Gradually I learned how to steer by the sails. I thought it would take me twenty days to get to Port Elizabeth. But I was lucky with the winds – which were south, south-west and then north-west. It took me eleven days.' Nandor's story is typical of those who competed in The BOC Challenge 1990–91.

The race of 1990–91 was the third such single-handed classic. The first BOC Challenge in 1982–83 attracted seventeen starters from eight countries, there were four retirements, two yachts sank and one was destroyed after going aground. There were ten finishers.

In the second BOC in 1986–87, there were twenty-five starters from ten countries and sixteen completed the course. The event had been made possible since its inception by the support of The BOC Group, the world-wide company whose principal businesses are industrial gases, health care and high vacuum technology.

Philippe Jeantot, a true gentleman of France who has charmed practically everyone connected with The BOC Challenge, won the first race, completing the marathon with the specially designed *Credit Agricole* in 159 days, 2 hrs, 26 mins on 9 May 1983. It was his birthday. Sailing a new *Credit Agricole*, Jeantot won again in 1987, this time in 134 days, 5 hrs, 23 mins, 56 secs. Jeantot was back with a new boat, *Credit Agricole IV*, for the third race for which he was the pre-start favourite.

The original course, Newport, Cape Town, Sydney, Rio de Janeiro and back to Newport, had been changed for the third voyage. There had been much unhappiness among skippers about marine facilities during the halt in Rio in 1987, and the increasing crime-related problems of the city were another major factor in the decision to choose another staging port.

Coincidentally, the choice of Punta had been made at the recommendation of BOC's new Race Director, the American Mark Schrader. Mark, a veteran of the second BOC, which he completed with the 49-footer *Lone Star*, had been the first American to complete a circumnavigation via the five southernmost capes.

The 48 provisional entrants included ten skippers planning to return from the previous race; an Australian, Alby Burgin, whose ambition it was to celebrate his seventy-fifth birthday during the voyage; Brad van Liew, 22, an American who stood to be the youngest in the history of the event; Robin Knox-Johnston, the first to sail single-handed, non-stop around the world in 1968–69 and the former race chairman of The BOC Challenge; and three women. Alas, Burgin, van Liew, Knox-Johnston and one of the women failed to make even the next, fully-paid-up stage on the way to the start – as did a total of some sixteen others on the original list.

The fleet would be the most diverse, the most dedicated, in many ways the most interesting, and perhaps even the most unpredictable ever assembled. Schrader correctly predicted that about half the boats would be specially designed for the race, and that several of them would be capable of beating the records of the last race. He thought Class I, for boats over fifty foot up to sixty foot, would be won in under 125 days, and Class II, for yachts between 40–50 foot, in less than 140 days. The Corinthian class, for unsponsored entries, had the same, 40–50 foot, limits as Class II.

At London and New York press conferences, Schrader drew special attention to the unique safety features of the race, such as watertight bulkheads. Yachts had now to be fitted with radar and a sound guard – meaning it was possible for an electronic look-out to be maintained by all skippers at all times. Every craft had also to be fitted with the new 406 EPIRB (Emergency Position Indicating Radio Beacon) which can transmit a distress signal that can be quickly detected and accurately located anywhere in the world by COSPAS-SARSAT, the new international satellite search-and-rescue system.

As in previous races, the yachts would be fitted with ARGOS transponders to facilitate accurate positioning of the single-handers via satellite.

The transponders automatically transmit signals that relay the positions of the yachts several times daily to satellites which, in turn, pass the data to land-based computers. The decoded information is then passed to race administration.

The transponders can be removed to a life raft in an emergency and there is a 'panic button' that can be pressed to indicate via the satellites that immediate assistance is needed. The competitors were required also to make regular reports by radio to the BOC race headquarters in Newport.

At that first, January conference in London, thirteen entrants for the race were present. Only two Britons, Davie and Hall, were to make the starting line. Robin Davie, an extraordinary character whose fund-raising activities to reach The BOC Challenge include helping to build the new airfield in the Falklands; dodging Exocet missiles during the Iran–Iraq war in the Persian Gulf while working on a salvage tug; and then running something like thirteen marathons in ten days to raise sponsorship from local businessmen in Cornwall.

Hall, like Davie, was equally tireless if perhaps less reckless in his fundraising activities. He arranged for the rock group the Kinks to put on a concert as the culmination of a 10-day fundraising event that included cabarets, lottery competitions and even boxing-matches.

Seven of thirteen American entrants were at the New York conference. Only Hal Roth was to make it to the race start.

Among the other American entrants, Bill Gilmore, Floyd Romack and Paul Thackaberry, had boats nearing completion, while Mike Plant had the 60-foot *Duracell* he had built for the Globe Challenge. Jack Boye, a well-known single-hander from New York, joined the line-up late with *Project City Kids*, formerly the much proven *Tuesday's Child*. Jeantot had stated all along that he would not make a decision on the third BOC until he had completed the Globe race.

There were to be just six American starters, Boye, Gilmore, Hooke, Plant, Roth and Thackaberry; four Australian, David Adams, John Biddlecombe, Kanga Birtles and Don McIntyre; and five French entries, Isabelle Autissier, Christophe Auguin, Yves Dupasquier, Alain Gautier and Philippe Jeantot.

In January 1990, the other hopefuls were the three Japanese, Minoru Saito, Toshihitko Kawabata and Yukoh Tada; two Canadians, Marc Perron and Jane Weber; two South Africans, John Martin and Bertie Reed, and Dutchman Roel Engels who hoped to compete with the *Credit Agricole* that won the 1986–87 race. Neither Kawabata-san, Perron nor Engels were to make it.

As with the 1986 start, twenty-five boats were finally to set sail, although the boats from ten countries for the third BOC Challenge were generally rated to be of a higher overall competitive standard. With thirteen 60-footers competing in Class I, it was the most formidable line-up ever assembled for a single-handed voyage.

There were four 60-footers from France, namely, *Groupe Sceta*, sailed by Christophe Auguin; *Ecureuil Poitou-Charentes*, the entry of Isabelle Autissier, the only woman in the Class I line-up; *Generali Concorde*, being sailed by Alain Gautier; and *Credit Agricole IV*, sailed by Philippe Jeantot. The three Australian 60-footers were *Innkeeper*, skippered by David Adams; *Interox Crusader*, sailed by John Biddlecombe; and *Jarkan Yacht Builders*, the entry of Kanga Birtles. John Martin, sailing *Allied Bank*, and Bertie Reed, on *Grinaker*, were returning to the race from South Africa; the American Mike Plant, and *Duracell*, were the sole American combination in Class I; Nandor Fa and *Alba Regia* were the first Hungarian combination in the voyage in any category; other national firsts were Jose de Ugarte and *BBV Expo '92*, from Spain, and Enda O'Coineen and *Kilcullen* from Ireland. Returning for the third time were Jeantot and Reed; Biddlecombe, Martin and Plant were back for a second time.

The seven entered for Class II were the Frenchman Yves Dupasquier, with *Servant IV*; the Englishman Josh Hall with his *New Spirit of Ipswich*; Don McIntyre of Australia with *Sponsor Wanted*; the American Hal Roth, and his *Sebago*; Yukoh Tada from Japan with *Koden VIII*; and Jack Boye, USA, sailing *Project City Kids*; and Jane Weber, a Canadian and the first woman to enter for the third BOC, and her *Tilley Endurable*.

The unsponsored Corinthian fleet comprised Robin Davie and his *Global Exposure*; the Japanese Minoru Saito and *Shutendohji II*; and three Americans, Bill Gilmore with *Zafu*; Robert Hooke and his *Niihau 4*, and Paul Thackaberry with *Volcano*. None of the Corinthian entry had competed in an earlier BOC. Two of them, Davie and Thackaberry, had really hoped to raise sponsorship.

Eighteen skippers had managed to raise sponsorship, though for most of them it was only partial support. One of these was Don McIntyre, who said he had gone about £180,000 in debt to make the voyage. The cost of a well-equipped 60-footer for the third BOC ranged from around £120,000–900,000.

Two days before the start, McIntyre had the late fright of needing to find an extra £14,000 to insure *Sponsor Wanted*. This was because he borrowed almost £60,000 more to cover costs on his campaign which he put at more than £200,000. The additional £14,000 was to insure the £60,000 loan. It was to cost him £91 a day throughout the voyage to pay interest on his loans.

However, all but two of the twenty-five skippers who signified they would make the trip managed to reach Newport by the required deadline. The two latecomers were O'Coineen's *Kilcullen* and Gautier's *Generali Concorde*. The arrival of *Generali Concorde*, 16½ hours behind schedule, was to lead to the first, orchestrated controversy of the race. It came about because of Rule 14.2 of the Rules and Conditions of The BOC Challenge 1990–91, that states:

Any starters not there (Newport) by that time (1200 hrs local, September 1) will receive an hour-for-hour penalty for each hour the yacht is late. The penalty will be added to the total elapsed time for the first leg of the race.

Alain Gautier and a small number of the French press not surprisingly favoured the more familiar, French penalty of a fine. But the Race Committee were determined to stand by their rules unless they were shown to be incorrect or unenforceable. So, despite threats by the skipper that he would withdraw and compete in the Route du Rhum race, *Generali Concorde* started with a 16½-hour penalty – much less daunting than the 308½ hours suffered for the late arrival of Enda O'Coineen's *Kilcullen*.

O'Coineen, 34, an eccentric Irishman who had crossed the Atlantic in a 16-foot inflatable dinghy, decided, when it was too late to build a new boat for The BOC Challenge, to compete with a proven performer. Alas, delays and ill luck on his qualifying voyage meant he did not arrive in Newport until 8.30 a.m. on the morning of 14 September – just some 27½ hours before the race start at noon from Fort Adams.

It was far from the end of O'Coineen's problems. He decided to rerig the yacht, and by the time he had been passed by the inspection committee, it was a further five days before he sailed, at 5.35 p.m. local time. That night, nineteen miles off Point Judith, in southern Rhode Island, *Kilcullen* was in collision with a fishing-boat. The yacht's mast was broken in three places and the bow badly damaged, and, as a consequence of accepting a series of tows back to Newport that exceeded the permitted ten miles, O'Coineen was disqualified from the first leg.

The skippers who did make the start were the most experienced ever to line up for an ocean voyage. Their combined single-handed sea time added up to more than 850,000 miles or some thirty-two times around the world. Philippe Jeantot, who had sailed more than 25,000 miles before he started the first BOC Challenge in 1982–83, was competing in his fourth circumnavigation.

Right Philippe Jeantot, twice winner of The BOC Challenge, celebrates his arrival in Cape Town

2　A Proud History

Single-handed yacht racing began in 1960. There had been several earlier notable solo voyages as distinct from true racing, but it was the first single-handed transatlantic race, starting from Plymouth on 11 June 1960, that turned a cruising custom into a serious sport.

The first round-the-world race for solo sailors came eight years later. The prize was a Golden Globe, and £5,000 was put up by *The Sunday Times* newspaper. The rules allowed for yachts to start from anywhere at any time, and the prize went to the first to complete the unique voyage. There were a total of eight starters, but only one of them, Robin Knox-Johnston, completed the course.

It was another ten years before the plans were made for a second round-the-world race which was to become The BOC Challenge. There were seventeen starters from eight countries in that first race and with the four retirements and the loss of *Lady Pepperell*, *Skoiern* and *Gipsy Moth*, there were ten finishers. But it was to be widely acclaimed as a triumph, not least because of the outstanding acts of seamanship. Impressively, Philippe Jeantot was a week ahead of the opposition by Cape Town.

Tony Lush was to run into trouble on his way to victory on 27 November when *Lady Pepperell* was rolled. As the extent of the damage became clear, he put out a distress call that was picked up by Alistair Campbell, the ham who was making his name as a race monitor. Rob Koziomkowski, a ham in Newport, and David White aboard *Gladiator* in Cape Town, were to assist in the rescue co-ordination of Lush, who was advised by Francis Stokes to sail down on his *Mooneshine*, some fifty miles ahead.

It was an amazing feat of seamanship; one that was to epitomize the great spirit of The BOC Challenge. It was the first BOC rescue and demonstrated with great clarity the remarkable camaraderie that had developed between the skippers, and the intense enthusiasm and reliability of the race organizers and their supporting ham radio enthusiasts. There could not have been a better first example of BOC self-reliance and concern for all who competed in the first and the subsequent voyages.

It was on the third leg to Rio, on 9 February 1983, that there began the first ever rescue of a yachtsman in distress in the Southern Ocean between Australia and Cape Horn. It was to go down as one of the most remarkable feats of seamanship, navigation and perseverance in modern maritime history. The rescue, carried out about midway between Sydney and Cape Horn, in desolate wastes about 1,800 miles from anywhere, took some fifty-nine hours to complete. The protagonists were the Frenchman Jacques de Roux, whose yacht *Skoiern II* was sinking; the Englishman Richard Broadhead, the rescuer whose remarkable feat with *Perseverance of Medina* was to earn him the British Yachtsman of the Year award in 1984; with a supporting cast of BOC race officials and ham radio operators in a number of countries between the United States and Australia. There had been some concern for de Roux by two of his fellow competitors who had spoken with him the night before the rescue operation began. Sailing at some fifty-five degrees south, de Roux's evident worries about continual 55-knot winds and *Skoiern* taking in a lot of water had been noted by Broadhead and South African Bertie Reed. The three agreed to communicate the following morning.

But de Roux failed to make contact because by now *Skoiern* had pitchpoled. The Frenchman, lying in his quarter berth, felt the boat roll through 180°. Water poured in so fast that the change in pressure made his ears pop. Already suffering from exhaustion, he was now wet through, bleeding and bruised. His yacht was without a mast, her forward deck hatch had been ripped away and she floated with little more than four inches of air space under her deck. Each successive wave deposited more water below decks.

De Roux was left with little alternative but to activate the panic switch on his Argos transponder, and as he began pumping to keep *Skoiern* afloat, he hoped someone would get to him before it was too late. His distress signal reached the Argos decoding station two hours after de Roux activated the panic button, and the organizers in Newport were quickly alerted. The Frenchman's precise position was 55°29' south, 126°55' west, with *Skoiern* drifting in an easterly direction at about 1½ knots. The only immediate help near at hand was likely to be that provided by BOC competitors.

It was twelve hours before any contact was made. Ham enthusiast Matt Johnstone, in Owaka, New Zealand, had been monitoring the airwaves since being alerted by Koziomkowski, and he picked up Broadhead transmitting Bertie Reed's position to another ham and interrupted their transmission. On hearing the news, the Englishman turned immediately into the mountainous Southern Ocean swells to begin his search for *Skoiern*.

The problem for Broadhead, 'an old-fashioned' Englishman who talks in understatements, was that some of these satellite fixes were interspersed with dead-reckoning plots, and with nothing to differentiate between the two, the confusion over his own position eventually led him to ignore some of the information and plot his own course towards the stricken yachtsman.

Broadhead finally reached de Roux's reported position at 01.00 GMT on Friday, 11 February, 47 hours after being alerted. But he saw nothing of *Skoiern*. Thinking he must have sailed past the French yacht, Broadhead went below to discuss his next move over the radio. As he talked to his New Zealand contact, de Roux sighted *Perseverance* some fifty yards away. His elation turned to despair when the British yacht, her deck deserted, sailed on into the distance.

Broadhead came back on deck shortly before 02.00 GMT, having made himself a cup of tea. Searching the horizon, his eyes caught a flash of white about two miles in the distance. At first he thought it was an iceberg, then the bridge of a ship. Then, as a wave lifted *Skoiern* clear he realized it was the sail of her jury rig.

The rescue had been made just in time, for four hours later, with the winds gusting up to thirty-five knots, *Skoiern*'s Argos transponder stopped transmitting, indicating she had finally foundered. Discussing the rescue later in Rio, Broadhead was most impressed with how the quiet, popular de Roux had suddenly been able to speak 'perfect English.'

'I had never been able to talk to the chap, before,' said an amused Richard. 'He could say only a few words in English to me in Newport, Cape Town and Sydney. But when we fell down on the deck from the exhaustion of getting him aboard *Perseverance*, he suddenly found a wonderful command of the language.'

The rescue of de Roux – he was tragically to be lost at sea during the second BOC Challenge in 1986–87 – not only helped cement the communications arrangements for the race generally, but also the vital role of the international ham operators.

In the second BOC Challenge four years later, Jeantot won with the new *Credit Agricole III* in 134 days, 5 hrs, 23 mins, 56 secs, – some twenty-five days quicker than in 1982–83. There were twenty-five starters from ten countries and sixteen completed the course. Six – *Neptune's Express* (Richard McBride, New Zealand), *ACI Crusader* (John Biddlecombe, Australia), *Madonna* (Takao Shimada, Japan), *Quailo* (Mac Smith, US), *Miss Global* (Luis Tonizzo, US), and *Airforce* (Dick Cross, US) – did not complete the first leg to Cape Town.

The second leg to Sydney witnessed the worst accident of the race. The tragic loss of Jacques de Roux came some 250 miles from Sydney when the French naval officer, rescued so dramatically four years earlier, had seemed set to win the second leg as Mike Plant, his closest pursuer, was then some eighty-five miles astern.

There was early concern for the well-being of de Roux. Argos reports over a 24-hour period showed the route being sailed by *Skoiern* to be so unusual that there was concern that all was not well with the skipper. He was last seen on deck by the crew of a passing yacht on 18 December. Two days later his yacht was found unoccupied.

From the evidence on board, a half-eaten meal, none of the safety gear or waterproof clothing missing, it was suspected the Frenchman had gone on deck in a hurry and slipped over the side. It was believed at the time that the yacht might have gone aground shortly before the accident, which would have accounted for a jammed rudder, damage that de Roux had not reported.

The loss of de Roux merely confirmed what everyone associated with the race had always known: that in such a daring adventure, an accident such as that which befell the skipper of *Skoiern IV* could occur at any time during the 27,000-mile voyage. Indeed, there was surprise in the world of serious single-handers that there had not been the loss of life earlier in the history of The BOC Challenge. Certainly the loss of de Roux would not diminish the desire of this type of single-handed seafarer to continue to compete in such daunting events.

If the rescue of Jacques de Roux by Richard Broadhead was the outstanding example of seamanship in the first race, the self-determination and self-reliance of Canadian John Hughes in saving himself was the finest example in the second race. On 6 February 1987, his boat, *Joseph Young* was dismasted some 1,500 miles from New Zealand and 4,000 miles from Cape Horn. Hughes sailed some 4,400 miles to East Cove, East Falkland, in forty-five days under jury rig. He was to be honoured by the Single-handed Hall of Fame in Newport for his achievement, remarkable by any standards.

Right   Hal Roth, at sixty-three the oldest competitor in the race and veteran of the 1986 BOC Challenge

3   *New and Familiar Faces*

Sports halls of fame are an American phenomenon. Most are national. But at least two, both based in Newport, Rhode Island, are international. They are the International Tennis Hall of Fame, and the International Single-Handed Hall of Fame, established only in 1986.

The BOC Group provided the initial funding for the hall, Richard Giordano, the BOC Chairman and Chief Executive dedicated the hall, and The BOC Group underwrote various improvements and a gala opening on the eve of The BOC Challenge 1990–91. This occasion also featured the induction of Philippe Jeantot, who so dominated the first two BOC races and more than any other person helped to popularize the event. He was not the first BOC sailor to be so honoured, that distinction having gone to the Canadian John Hughes for his outstanding feat of seamanship in The BOC Challenge 1986–87.

In winning The BOC Challenge 1982–83 with his uniquely radical *Credit Agricole*, Philippe inspired a new approach to single-handed sailing that transformed short-handed racing.

Having initiated his own, non-stop circumnavigation race in 1989, it was perhaps remarkable that he was still ready to compete for the third time in The BOC Challenge. 'My most important motivation is the pleasure of sailing around the world solo,' he said, when asked about his decision to battle again around the world in a yacht. 'This pleasure does not fade with the years, but grows. Competing on more and more sophisticated and powerful boats makes the race a new challenge. Preparing the boat is a captivating and fascinating experience for me. It's at this stage that one puts one's know-how and experience to use. Afterwards, when sailing, one must prove that one made the right technical choices.

'The BOC Challenge is the consummate route, and there's the bonus of the South Seas at the other end. Seeing the 40th parallel waves again is such a great pleasure in itself that one needs no other motivation for undertaking the trip.'

Bertie Reed, like Philippe returning for his third BOC, had also competed in the French

Globe Challenge. One of the characters of solo racing, Reed was initially optimistic about his prospects for the third BOC, having secured valuable sponsorship from Grinaker, the South African electronics company.

Plant, returning for his second successive BOC, had the Rodger Martin-designed *Duracell*. He had raced the Martin-designed *Airco Distributor* that won Class II in The BOC Challenge 1986–87. Plant had secured valuable sponsorship from Duracell, first for the Globe Challenge and then The BOC Challenge.

For four months before the start of the BOC, Plant and his shoreside team made a number of changes to *Duracell* to refine and improve performance.

Another confident starter was John Martin, with a £235,000 incentive to win. The prize was offered by Allied Bank, his sponsor, for winning each of the four stages.

Hal Roth, living in Portsmouth, Rhode Island, wanted to do his second BOC in a new 60-footer, but he didn't find the financing to realize his ambition. Instead, with backing from Sebago, the footwear manufacturers, he set about modifying *American Flag*, the Bill Lee-designed 50-footer he sailed in the second BOC. He fitted the yacht with ballast tanks, changed the mast and rig, and considerably lightened the yacht.

Roth was a returnee to Class II, like the Japanese skipper Yukoh Tada. Born in 1930, Tada-san was the victor in Class II in the first BOC. In 1990 he came to the start with *Koden VIII*, which he designed and helped build himself. Tada-san's story this time was to have a tragic ending.

Two other skippers, Nandor Fa with *Alba Regia* and Paul Thackaberry with *Volcano*, built their 1990–91 BOC boats. Yves Dupasquier joined with four friends and formed the company called Looping which built his boat, *Servant IV*, and Mike Plant directed and helped to build *Duracell*.

Kanga Birtles with his *Jarkan Yacht Builders*, John Martin with *Allied Bank*, and Don McIntyre with *Sponsor Wanted* each own yacht-building companies that constructed their BOC boats.

Eleven yachts were built specifically for The BOC Challenge 1990–91. They were *Alba Regia*, *Koden VIII*, *Volcano*, *Servant IV*, *Jarkan Yacht Builders*, *Allied Bank*, *Sponsor Wanted*, *Shutendohji II* (Minoru Saito), *Groupe Sceta* (Christopher Auguin), *Zafu* (Bill Gilmore) and *Niihau 4* (Robert Hooke). Three of them, *Zafu*, a J-44 sloop; *Niihau 4*, a Ron Holland-designed Dekiri 45-footer, and *Shutendohji II*, an Adams 50-foot cutter, came from standard production lines but were modified for the BOC Challenge.

A further four that were to compete in the third BOC were built for the second race four years previously. They were *Interox Crusader* (John Biddlecombe), formerly named *ACI Crusader*; *New Spirit of Ipswich* (Josh Hall), formerly *Airco Distributor*; *Kilcullen* (Enda O'Coineen), formerly named *Thursday's Child*; and *BBV Expo '92* (José de Ugarte), the former *Ecureuil d'Aquitaine* that was runner-up in the 1986–87 event.

By general consensus, the most interesting and radical starter was to be Yves Dupasquier's 50-footer *Servant IV*, a lightweight craft made for a tough, determined crew and believed by a number of skippers to be 'the way BOC boats will go'.

For the more technically minded, the yacht, designed by Jean Beret, has a beam of 13 ft, 1in and a draft of 8 ft, 7 in. *Servant IV* displaces 12,125 lb; she has no furlers; the mast is well for'ard and fractionally rigged, and the No. 1 is sheeted for'ard of the shrouds. Dupasquier had no overlapping headsails and, to keep the weight down, his inventory of headsails was just a No. 1, a spare No. 1 and a storm jib. His very big mainsail, with massive roach, is more commonly associated with a catamaran.

Yves had chased weight to the extreme. He would not have a ghetto-blaster aboard

Philippe Jeantot in *Credit Agricole III* winning The BOC Challenge 1986–87

because it weighed 4 kg. It took a month to make the carbon-fibre rudder stocks, each of which weigh just 5 kg. He had just two glass-fibre benches jutting out of the sides of the hull to sit on; there was no steel in the chainplates, which were really glass-fibre glassed in.

'It's cheap, it's fun to sail, it's safe and human,' said *Servant*'s skipper. 'It's very comfortable for me, though I can understand that when people first see *Servant* she seems "special".'

'All the electronics are concentrated in the same place, it means there is less wire and less weight. The electronics are tracked across before water ballast is taken on. There are two 700-litre ballast tanks at the rear, but I seldom use more than 200 litres per tank.'

A delightfully frank, intelligent man with a self effacing sense of humour, Yves was brought up in Gergovie, near Clermont-Ferrand in the Central Massif region. He had never put a foot on a boat until 1980 when he was in Morocco and found himself on one absolutely by chance. 'They needed a crew to sail to the West Indies. Though I had no experience, I convinced them to take me on,' he said.

His subsequent experiences included twelve transatlantic voyages, two of them in Mini-Transats for yachts of 26 foot and in 1984 he won his class in the Quebec–St Malo classic with the 50-foot catamaran, *Santal*. For the 1987 Mini-Transat, he built and raced *Servant Soft*. He was a member of the team that built *Ecureuil d'Aquitaine* for Titouan Lamazou for The BOC Challenge 1986–87.

Dupasquier gathered four boat-building, hang-gliding friends and formed a company called Looping, whose sole purpose was building The BOC Challenge yacht. The company was named for their favourite hang-gliding stunt, the 'boucle de boucle' or loop-the-loop.

'Sailing and hang-gliding have a lot in common,' said Yves. 'Only water is thicker than air.'

Servant 4 was a stretched Mini-Transat boat. Yves considers the BOC an extended Mini-Transat. The boat would not 'work' as a 60-footer, though that is what was contemplated when building began.

'The 50-footer is just the beginning,' he says. 'It's not very good upwind, though I was doing 8 knots to the 8.5 knots of 60-footers, but we can do better. I went to Jean Beret because he was the designer of my Mini-Transat boat. I spoke to five designers before I settled on Jean.

For perseverence, the effort of Paul Thackaberry, the American entrant from Oxford, Michigan, took some beating among the 1990–91 skippers. After five years of a practically all-consuming effort, he had succeeded at his second attempt to make the start.

The 38-year-old tool-and-die-maker had hoped to compete in The BOC Challenge 1986–87. Having failed to achieve that goal he designed and built the 50-foot cutter *Volcano* – named after the Jimmy Buffet song – for the third BOC. 'I started building *Volcano* when the maxis were delaminating during their 1985–86 round-the-world race,' he says. 'So I decided to avoid foam and choose cedar.' This led to *Volcano* being constructed of fibreglass and epoxy over a stripped cedar core. 'Because I couldn't afford design fees, I tried to copy everything,' he grins. In fact, his twin rudder 'design' is an imitation of the type developed for The BOC Challenge 1986–87 by Jeantot.

Uniquely in the history of The BOC Challenge, two women were in the Newport line-up for the first time, Jane Weber, 45, of Canada, the first to enter, and Isabelle Autissier, 33, of France. Isabelle, sailing *Ecureuil Poitou-Charentes*, said she was taking part for 'self-improvement,' while Jane, whose yacht is *Tilley Endurable*, gave 'challenging herself' as her reason for entering the marathon circumnavigation.

NEW AND FAMILIAR FACES

Isabelle, who lives at La Rochelle, on the west coast of France, began competitive sailing as part of her quest for self-improvement. The Frenchwoman has a penchant for solo sailing: 'Alone, one is obliged to give absolutely all that one can give. It's powerful.'

At 11,000 lb, *Koden VIII* was the lightest boat in the fleet. She was designed by her skipper Yukoh Tada

Paul Thackaberry's BOC Challenge was a stalwart performance based on five years of preparations

Corinthian Robin Davie on *Global Exposure* engaged in the endless round of maintenance and repair

A delighted Josh Hall reaches Sydney. His injured right knee required immediate surgery

Sponsor Wanted no longer. Don and Margie McIntyre rechristen the yacht *Buttercup* in Sydney

Hal Roth, at work on *Sebago* in Sydney

Skipper's-eye-view: Don McIntyre surveys the scene aboard *Buttercup*

Yves Dupasquier's Class II *Servant IV* is dwarfed by the beamy *Groupe Sceta* which is over a metre wider than rival Class I entry *Jarkan Yacht Builders* (*right*)

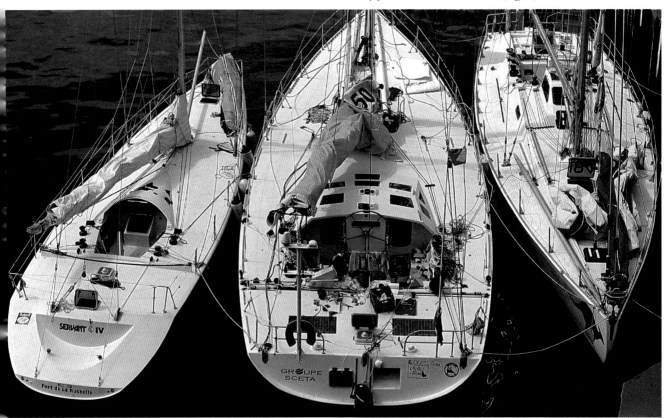

Left David Adams' *Innkeeper* was borrowed for the race, and modified for single-handling

Briton Josh Hall in Sydney. His injured knee was fitted with a state-of-the-art brace
for the third leg of the race to Punta del Este

Jarkan Yacht Builders at the Sydney restart

BBV Expo '92 had a proven BOC pedigree – she finished second in the previous race as *Ecureuil d'Aquitaine*

Punta del Este: *Duracell* and Mike Plant arrive in fourth place on 8 March

Bertie Reed's *Grinaker*. This race was to be Bertie's farewell to single-handling

Yves Dupasquier's *Servant IV* – described by Josh Hall as 'a 60-footer in disguise'

Like his first attempt, John Biddlecombe's second BOC was to end prematurely

4   *Disappointments and Triumphs*

Crowds of delighted wellwishers greet Isabelle Autissier as she arrives in
Cape Town

The start was near perfect, the first stage was closer and more absorbing than for any such ocean race. The opening stage of the race was not without incident, there was some controversy, some damage and four retirements, but the camaraderie, the companionship, enthusiasm and genuine praise confirmed that The BOC Challenge had increased in stature.

The fleet of twenty-four, minus late arrival Enda O'Coineen and *Kilcullen*, had made a spectacular, prompt start in bright sunshine and a light westerly at noon on Saturday, 15 September, just after Newport had been engulfed by a downpour of tropical dimensions.

There was a new start line, from Fort Adams, and the early leader, out past the Brenton Reef Tower, was *Duracell*, sailed by Mike Plant.

Unknown to many of the thousands lining the Fort Adams shore, the banks of Narragansett Bay's East Passage or watching from the large spectator fleet, the start was not without its problems. Josh Hall's *New Spirit of Ipswich* brushed with *Duracell* on the start line, and Nandor Fa's *Alba Regia* suffered some damage after collisions with John Martin's *Allied Bank* and David Adams' *Innkeeper*. Indeed, *Alba Regia* was holed and Nandor had the extra unwanted problem from the start until Cape Town of having to bail out about twenty buckets of water a day. Worse, within an hour of the start, Paul Thackaberry's *Volcano*, was being towed back to Newport minus a rudder. It had been pulled out after becoming entangled with a lobster-pot.

Significantly, in terms of a performance indicator, four French yachts, *Groupe Sceta*, *Generali Concorde*, *Ecureuil Poitou-Charentes* and *Servant IV* were the narrow leaders as skippers completed their first twenty-four hours at sea.

Next, on Day 2, it was Bertie Reed, on the most westerly heading with the best average speed of 10.2 knots, who became the pacemaker.

On Day 3, David Adams edged ahead to lead Reed by about seven miles. The group immediately astern of Reed's *Grinaker* included *Generali Concorde* and *Groupe Sceta*. *Servant IV*, right at the front, led Class II from *New Spirit of Ipswich*, while Bill Gilmore and *Zafu* led the Corinthian Class from Robin Davie's *Global Exposure*.

It was after only four days that *Generali Concorde, Groupe Sceta* and *Credit Agricole IV* took up the pacemaking they were to maintain to a larger degree to the end of the leg. There were supporting roles, but it was Alain Gautier of *Concorde*, Christophe Auguin of *Sceta* and Philippe Jeantot of *Credit* who were the stars.

Meanwhile, on Day 5, as a tropical depression 850 miles east of the Leeward Isles and travelling north-west at 35 knots loomed as a possible threat, there were two more 'casualties.' John Biddlecombe and Bill Gilmore joined Enda O'Coineen on the 'concerned' list.

Biddlecombe was headed for Bermuda, where he had made an emergency stop at the start of the 1986–87 voyage because of a groin injury. The Australian, making only 1.6 knots, reported that all of his auto-pilots had failed and he was diverting to Bermuda to collect spares or effect repairs.

Meanwhile, O'Coineen's dismasted *Kilcullen* was being towed back to Newport, and Gilmore, who had been overtaken by *Global Exposure* was radioing his wife Emmy that he had decided to quit the race he had expected would take him 150 days to complete.

The retirement of Gilmore, a pleasant, humorous American who had promised to become the philosopher of the fleet, was a big surprise. The reasons for his retirement were 'complex and a bit obscure, even to me.' He wrote: 'At the bottom line, however, I quit because for me, it [the race] has ceased to be fun.' He said he had been away from home for the best part of three years in preparation for the BOC and other races. He missed his family, and had little time to read. He had not been sailing well; he felt he had even been incautious with regards to safety. 'It is best that I retire,' he said. 'There are friends I'd like to see in the Caribbean, and I haven't been skiing with my sons in too many years.'

It was during the fifth week at sea that John Biddlecombe, the best-sponsored of the Australians, with a reputed $A500,000 backing, announced he was abandoning the race and returning to Bermuda. He had a rudder problem. It was thought that his withdrawal would do little to help single-handers secure sponsorship in Australia.

It was as skippers began their second week at sea that troubles began. *Grinaker* hit a whale; *Alba Regia* suffered a broken gooseneck; *BBV Expo '92* had ballast-tank problems and a faulty radio; Auguin's radio failed; Mike Plant had minor ballast-tank leaks, and Robert Hooke had an engine problem. So, in time, did Plant. His generator, which somehow was sucking in air, would not take in fuel automatically, forcing the American skipper to refuel from a jug. Indeed, he was to 'run the whole race out of a gallon milk jug', as he put it. At one stage Mike's generator was out of action for three days, during which time the American had no electrics. 'It would not,' he joked, 'have done for *Duracell* to have been without power.' Power problems were also to trouble Isabelle Autissier, who said the generator failed the first day out of Newport. After that she had only solar panels. 'It meant I could use my auto-pilot for only twelve hours a day, and one small computer for weather.'

David Adams was to suffer a broken gooseneck and run out of diesel, and Nandor Fa listed a loose rudder stock, broken furling gear and a host of lesser problems as first-leg setbacks.

In Class II, Josh Hall had the sat-nav fail on his *New Spirit of Ipswich* the first day out of Newport; later in the voyage his generator 'blew up' and he lost the use of his auto-pilots. Yukoh Tada's breakages included his backstay and one of his bow stabilizers.

On the second day out of Newport, Hal Roth lost his new mainsail; three weeks into the voyage he broke two chainplates. 'I thought that was the end of it,' he said. 'I didn't think I would be able to rerig the mast. But I cut some wire and with that and the terminal fitting I managed to stabilize the rig.'

Meanwhile, notable among the second week's better performances were to be the rapid improvement to fourth place of *Allied Bank* and, in Class II, the better placing of *Project City Kids*.

As the fleet began their third week, it was the familiar figure of Philippe Jeantot who was in his accustomed place at the front as the yachts began to emerge from the Doldrums. Jeantot had opened a useful, 77-mile lead on Plant, with Martin a mere four miles back in third place.

The story of the fourth week was about John Martin catching and passing Philippe Jeantot, and the development of a titanic struggle between the top dozen or so competitors. The closeness of the competition was unique in the history of The BOC Challenge. So was the absence of really serious, race-stopping problems and really extreme weather conditions.

But as Martin was reporting 'no problems' with *Allied Bank*, Thackaberry told AT & T's High Seas Radio Whisky Oscar Mike (WOM) in Fort Lauderdale that the bow of his *Volcano* was delaminating and his for'ard compartment was half-full of water. That was on 5 October. A day later he had 'fixed it,' though he faced further difficulties because he was out of propane gas.

Paul Thackaberry had perhaps the simplest standard seafaring recipe of all the skippers in the race: a can of rice, a can of soup and a can of water. 'I throw the contents of all three into a pan. When you heat it, it doesn't taste very good, but it adds substance and it doesn't fall off the plate!' Without any gas for cooking, he was to eat cold food for another 40 days.

On 5 October, Don McIntyre said he had the unnerving experience – not unusual at sea these days – of a freighter with no one apparently on watch crossing within five hundred yards of the bow of *Sponsor Wanted*.

Don's *Sponsor Wanted* was at this stage second in Class II to *City Kids*, which had taken the lead on the thirteenth night out. By now, 2,481 miles from Cape Town, Boye had a tidy, 347-mile lead over *Sponsor Wanted*. *Servant* was third, 489 miles behind Boye.

Global Exposure was still the Corinthian leader by 158 miles from *Volcano*. Davie was in good spirits. 'It's looking good,' he said. 'The boat is moving better now we've got a bit more wind. The Doldrums were very hard work. I'm now looking for fair winds to Cape Town.'

It was during the fifth week that the Newport–Cape Town stage turned into a gripping saga as Alain Gautier, reclaimed the lead. Gautier, who had sailed some 700 miles further and gone deeper into the Southern Ocean than any of the leaders, crossed the Table Bay line at 3.12 GMT on Tuesday, 24 October. The young Frenchman looked tired but fit and well, despite the exertions of three days without sleep.

Generali and Alain finished in the record time of 37 days, 11 hrs, 12 mins, 39 secs, which beat by 4 days, 13hrs, 57 mins, 57 secs, the previous best time of 42 days, 1 hr, 10 mins, 36 secs by John Martin and *Tuna Marine* in The BOC Challenge 1986–87. After that, for the first time in the history of the race, there were to be three more finishers within ten hours. This showed that marine technology had so improved that, even over a 7,000-mile voyage, there was little difference in performance capabilities.

Christophe Auguin and *Groupe Sceta* were second at noon local time, less than seven hours behind Gautier; John Martin's *Allied Bank* was third into Cape Town some 1¾

Spectator boats at Newport bid farewell to Don McIntyre and *Sponsor Wanted*

hours behind Auguin, and Philippe Jeantot and *Credit Agricole IV* arrived at 15.11 local time.

Because of Gautier's 16½-hour penalty, Auguin was declared the Class I winner, Martin was promoted to second, Jeantot to third with Gautier relegated to fourth. Understandably dismayed about the penalty, imposed for the late arrival of *Generali Concorde* in Newport for pre-race scrutineering, Alain expressed himself well pleased with the performance of his yacht and believed he had made only three mistakes on the voyage. Privately he agreed that arriving late at Newport was 'one of the three mistakes'; his second was the method by which he approached the Doldrums; and the third, the misjudgement of trying too hard. 'If I had been more cautious I might have made an even better time to Cape Town and not lost my spinnaker,' he said.

Auguin suffered many 'niggling technical problems' on the first half of the voyage to the Doldrums; the main problem for Martin, was losing all of his communications, including weatherfax and Argos reports, ten days out of Cape Town.

Just as the excitement was mounting for the arrival of the winner in Cape Town, Jane Weber announced that she was diverting to Recife with problems aboard *Tilley Endurable* that included a torn headsail and broken generator. The Canadian yachtswoman said she was also suffering from back pains. The following day it was reported that Jane was heading for Barbados.

Meanwhile, it was two more days before Mike Plant and Kanga Birtles hove into Table Bay. The time for Plant and *Duracell* was 39 days, 11 hrs, 41 mins, 40 secs; Birtles and *Jarkan* followed in 39 days, 16 hrs, 5 mins, 32 secs. Isabelle Autissier became the first woman skipper to complete the opening stage with *Ecureuil Poitou-Charentes* in 41 days, 4 hrs, 37 mins, 13 secs, at 10.44 p.m. on 27 October. The Frenchwoman, who celebrated her thirty-fourth birthday at sea, said the worst point of the voyage was being becalmed for three days; the worst problem was the loss through damage of a favourite spinnaker. Like the six finishers before her, Isabelle's time was well inside *Tuna Marine*'s record.

The first stage was completed with the arrival of Robert Hooke's *Niihau 4* at 17.37 GMT on 18 November. His time, not the slowest in BOC race history, was 64 days, 1 hr, 37 mins, 44 secs. Beset by problems that began just two days after the start, *Niihau* crossed the Table Bay finish line just a little more than six hours after the Japanese Minoru Saito's *Shutenendohji II*.

Robert Hooke immediately denied a report that had appeared in the London *Times* that he would be withdrawing from the voyage, and by early the following morning he was already at work with a number of helpers preparing *Niihau* for the next stage to Sydney. It epitomized the spirit of the BOC.

Right   Christophe Auguin celebrates his arrival at Cape Town where his
time of 37 days, 18 hrs, put him in first place

5 Leading Quartet

As skippers prepared for the start on 24 November of the second leg, the widely held belief was that the race winner would come from *Groupe Sceta, Allied Bank, Credit Agricole IV* or *Generali Concorde*, the first four in Cape Town.

There were other skippers, like Mike Plant, Kanga Birtles, Isabelle Autissier and perhaps Nandor Fa or Jose de Ugarte, who believed they might feature prominently on the second stage. Certainly Yves Dupasquier was fancied by some to beat some of the 60-footers across the Southern Ocean. Few believed, however, that anything but ill luck would prevent one of the four 'top guns' – Auguin, Martin, Jeantot and Gautier – each sailing 'fat' boats from claiming eventual victory in Newport.

Most of the second-leg leaders went to around 57° south. *Allied Bank* was first to find the westerlies.

After stating the previous evening that he would not be taking any chances, Philippe had the best start of the eighteen yachts that set off on time for Sydney in bright sunshine and an 18-knot southerly. Two Corinthians, Thackaberry and Saito-san, intentionally delayed their start to attend to repairs, while, because of a collision, Bertie Reed returned to port before the start: prefaced by a jet flypast and watched by a 700-boat spectator fleet.

Duracell, which had a bump at the Newport start, was again in collision, this time with *Grinaker*. Acknowledging that the mishap, some twenty minutes before the start, was his fault, Bertie returned to Cape Town for hasty repairs to the bowsprit, a chainplate, the forestay and the retensioning of *Grinaker*'s rigging. The yacht was back at sea in two hours and Bertie had caught up with the fleet by daybreak the next day.

Mike Plant, with a hole in *Duracell*'s starboard side and all of his for'ard starboard stanchions demolished, radioed he was taking in about fifty gallons of water an hour and would try to effect repairs when he found flatter conditions. He did make repairs, but he continued to take in about fifty gallons of water an hour. He said at the Sydney finish it had made no difference to his performance.

Saito-san and *Shutendohji II*, and *Volcano* and Paul Thackaberry, sailed on 26 November, by which time John Martin was well on his way to establishing a telling lead.

107

Josh Hall led Class II with *New Spirit of Ipswich* and Robert Hooke was top Corinthian with *Niihau 4*. Robert was later to report that his auto-pilot had failed a day out of Cape Town and that sailing by windvane had not been very efficient downwind.

'I began like a bull in a china shop,' said Martin. 'I had become very hyped in Cape Town. I had a very good beat down the coast towards Cape Point. *Allied Bank* beats well and I know the coast. By sunset on the first day I couldn't see anyone. By daybreak the second day I was in a very good position. I was headed east of south slightly, towards Sydney, making 7–8 knots. I was pretty happy.'

John, who in Sydney was to extol the practice of professional yachtsmen using all of the technical advice available, including weather routers, was by Day 4 heading the fleet at 44.25° south, 25.26° east. Behind him, as he made better than nine knots, the order was *Innkeeper*, *Groupe Sceta* and *Jarkan*, though Kanga Birtles, admitting he did 'not sail as well as possible', was to fall behind. Equally significant, especially to Martin who had expected Philippe to provide the 'main opposition', was the poor placing of *Credit Agricole*.

It was two days later, when his first spinnaker blew out, that Martin was indeed confirmed to be into the strong westerlies. He then began a series of regular daily runs of from 270–280 miles. 'I was averaging 11½–12 knots,' said John. 'It was a very comfortable, manageable speed.' It was more than that; it was a race winning speed following a race winning start.

Things were not going so well for everyone in the fleet. Three skippers, Nandor Fa, Hal Roth and Jack Boye had already had their ambitions blunted with equipment failures during the second week. Three others, Paul Thackaberry, Jose Ugarte and Don McIntyre had had collisions with whales. McIntyre also suffered a knockdown. Nandor was to report the crippling loss of rudders from *Alba Regia* and his decision to head for Port Elizabeth for repairs; Hal Roth was forced to turn back for Cape Town with water in his generator oil and further mast problems; and Boye reported forestay problems aboard *Project City Kids*.

It was on 1 December, just seven days into the leg, that Jose de Ugarte beat everyone with two frights in twenty-four hours. First, he had the whale bounce along the side of *BBV Expo '92*, and then later, in a turbulent sea when the yacht was caught with sails aback, Jose had his two auxiliary rudders washed away.

The whale frightened him most. 'It was a hell of a shock,' he said. 'I was doing 11–12 knots. I was thrown out of my seat. The boat stopped dead. I was very worried. I was afraid something was broken. But everything looked fine.'

By the following day, eight days out of Cape Town, *Allied Bank* enjoyed a comfortable, 215-mile lead over *Innkeeper*, Martin's closest rival. A day later the gap was some 240 miles over *Innkeeper*, with *Generali Concorde* 255 miles back and *Groupe Sceta* some 283 miles astern.

A week later, by which time it was expected *Allied Bank* could be in Sydney by 19 December, the gap was 340 miles, though John Martin was now hand-steering 'most of the time.' Seven of his eight auto-pilots had failed. Behind him were *Generali Concorde*; *Groupe Sceta*, 348 miles back; *Innkeeper*, 455 and *Credit Agricole IV*, 534. It was an astonishing lead built with singular singlemindedness.

The problems of the week during which Martin had virtually ensured victory included three knockdowns for *Koden VIII*; *Shutendohji*'s loss of a spinnaker in 70-knot winds; a lost spinnaker for *Duracell*; a torn mainsail for *Global Exposure*; and the development of a leak around *Niihau 4*'s rudder assembly.

Then, on 12 December, The BOC Challenge safety net was alerted world-wide when the

406 EPIRB on *New Spirit of Ipswich* was activated in 40-knot winds and 'a very nasty sea'. The alarm, unnecessary as it transpired, came when *Spirit* suffered a serious knockdown and the EPIRB was washed overboard and activated.

Within five minutes, the alarm had been picked up by satellite and acted upon world-wide. Simultaneously, the skippers' own 'safety net', the inter-yacht radio scheds that have been a feature of The BOC Challenge since it was first run, was also active.

Josh Hall called fellow skipper Don McIntyre who in turn reported through Sydney radio that all was 'OK' on *Spirit*. Josh suffered more than his yacht: the skipper dislocated his right knee. It was an old rugby injury, and though the knee was promptly put back, the British skipper could not put any weight on his leg for a week. 'I was scudding about on my backside for a week,' said Josh. 'And though Don McIntyre and Jack Boye told me I should rest, I went straight up on deck and put up all sail all I could. There was no way I was going to give up the lead I had gained.'

Yukoh Tada, bringing up the rear of Class II with his *Koden VIII* some 550 miles behind *Spirit*, was meanwhile knocked down three times during the night. Tada-san went off the air when he was explaining his misfortunes to Alistair Campbell by ham radio and he had a serious steering problem from then until he reached Sydney. Minoru Saito was at this time reporting 70-knot winds.

Paul Thackaberry, who said he had lost five auto-pilots but was 'OK', was one of the first of the skippers to complain of the cold – though later he was to enthuse about the icebergs he passed. 'They were enormous and looked beautiful – some were 300 feet high and one was eight miles long.' He was then at 59° 59′ south, 91° 46′ east.

Isabelle, who also had steering problems and spent twelve hours a day outside without heating, said she wore as many as seven layers of clothing. 'It was tough on the hands and feet,' she recalled. 'I used to put my feet in hot water for comfort when I came inside out of the cold.'

She would spend four hours steering in the stern, go inside for thirty minutes to have hot chocolate or soup or tea, and then return to her tiller. 'In fact,' she laughed, 'I ate all the time; chocolate, crackers. I was hungry all the time. I would have a cereal breakfast, a big lunch and a big dinner.' She also sang all the time she was on the tiller: 'All sorts of songs. I have music on board and I like to listen to it. But I have no outside speaker so I couldn't listen to it on the Southern Ocean leg.'

White-haired Jose de Ugarte, second oldest in the fleet also found it 'very cold' on the second leg. 'I began the leg with an old gas heater, but it packed up,' he explained. 'Most of the time it was 4°. That's like your fridge at home. Even my olive oil and eggs froze. I wore two thick pairs of socks – the first thigh high; thermal underwear; a woollen shirt; a polar suit and two jerseys.'

Jose, whose regular radio links with Bertie Reed became one of the most amusing daily occurrences for the skippers, also ate a lot. 'I would have a good breakfast of cereals, eggs, bacon and sausages. Then a mild lunch of perhaps fish and salad and cheese and crackers, and a big, cooked dinner. I had lots of stews with a lot of corned beef. I was averaging about 4,000–5,000 calories a day,' he said.

It was on the second leg, while he was off the Kerguelen Islands, that Jose's second grandson was born. 'I call him "Kergie",' said his grandfather, who was later to suffer a broken daggerboard on *BBV* and provide the biggest fright of the Cape Town–Sydney leg.

The loss overboard of the ARGOS transponder, unknown to *BBV*'s skipper or race control, came in the early hours of 24 December and raised immediate fears for the safety

Wall-to-wall high technology at *Allied Bank*'s nav station

of Jose. All that was clear was that the yacht remained close to stationary for several hours about fifty miles south-east of Gabo Island as Jose apparently failed to meet some of his radio scheds. While an airsearch was being made, Bertie Reed called from *Grinaker* with the news that he had been in contact with Jose. Jose later called race headquarters to explain he had been unable to maintain his regular radio scheds because of bad propagation (transmission) during the night, and he had not missed the transponder.

Earlier in the race, on 13 December, *Credit Agricole* moved into fourth place, gaining a slender, 17-mile advantage over *Innkeeper* in the process. David Adams was furious at losing what had been a lead of some 500 miles over Philippe.

On the following day, the rudderless *Alba Regia* reached Port Elizabeth. The replacement rudders were to arrive two days later and Nandor departed on 20 December.

Two days after Nandor tied up in Port Elizabeth, *Allied Bank* had closed to within 1,000 miles of Sydney. But it briefly seemed that the finish might be closer than expected as the pursuing French trio of Auguin, Gautier and Jeantot picked up speed to close on Martin.

Poor Jack Boye was at this time heading northwards in search of better weather conditions to effect repairs and reporting a broken spreader, the loss of all forward halyards and the inability to set a headsail on *Project City Kids*.

On 16 December Hal Roth arrived in Cape Town with the disabled *Sebago*. The next day, Christophe Auguin had closed to within 200 miles of Martin, then 747 miles from the finish. John had also had a nasty crash gybe, during which the boom swung across the cockpit three times. The third time, the mainsheet became entangled in a winch and pulled it clear of its mounting. *Allied Bank* was to enter the Bass Strait at 6.30 a.m. local time on 18 December, John having again extended his lead to 310 miles.

'When I got up to a 370-mile lead I was very wary,' recalled John. 'I knew how quickly I could lose even that lead if I made a mistake or got into a "hole". When I was down to just one auto-pilot I had to watch the course continually. I got very nervous about throwing away the lead. If the one auto-pilot had failed I knew I would have been in really big trouble.'

It was as John was entering the Bass Strait, as a result of a bad accident involving the involuntary gybing of *Generali Concorde*'s boom, that Alain Gautier probably lost whatever chance he might have had of catching the leader or finishing second. As Alain was checking from the port rails whether to gybe, the boom smashed into his back in an involuntary gybe and dragged the unfortunate Frenchman across the deck, into winches, and deposited him unconscious on the starboard rail. He said he could not move for thirty minutes after the accident. He was to spend the next twenty hours in his berth because he was too weak to move. Alain, who also hurt his hand, was to be down to mainsail only for a day because he could not handle a headsail. He discovered he had a nasty cut on his right hip and had lost quite a lot of blood. When he reached Sydney he was informed he had broken two small bones.

Alain, in company with *Groupe Sceta*, *Credit Agricole IV* and *Ecureuil Poitou-Charentes*, had chosen to go round the bottom of Tasmania *en route* to Sydney. The ploy failed to dislodge the leader, who on 19 December had closed to within 300 miles of the finish. But John, with a solid, 231-mile lead over Christophe, was frustrated at his slow progress in 3–5 knot winds. 'I went between King Island and Reed Rock – it's just a 10-mile gap – to find the wind,' said John. 'Fortunately, it came through as predicted at 18.00. So I went roaring through the Bass Strait at 11 knots. But I had to get east in 3–4 hours. I didn't make it. The average fell to 2 knots for two hours. Again the

gap closed and I was unable to get out to the east where the wind was.'

The South African finally crossed the Sydney line at 5.47 local time on 21 December to win in 26 days, 6 hrs, 47 mins, 23 secs, and lower the record for the stage by 2 days, 0 hrs, 25 mins, 59 secs. It was an impressive performance.

John, who collected a £41,000 bonus from Allied Bank for his leg victory and the $AS3,000 class award from the Commonwealth Industrial Gases Limited (CIG), the BOC host company in Sydney, said his worst moment was when he passed within five boat-lengths of a 'growler.' 'Those things bother me,' he said.

Christophe finished some eighteen hours behind John, and Alain became the third finisher a further three hours later.

But while the race to Sydney might have been won, the 7,000-mile stage from Cape Town was far from over, and surprises were still in store for skippers and organizers.

After it was reported from Cape Town on 22 December that Hal Roth had rejoined the race following repairs to *Sebago*, the disappointing news reached Sydney the following morning that *Ecureuil Poitou-Charentes* was dismasted off Tasmania, and *New Spirit of Ipswich* and *Sponsor Wanted* had each been knocked down three times in sustained 60-knot winds.

At the time of *Ecureuil*'s dismasting, Isabelle was lying sixth in the fleet. The mishap occurred at 40°07' south, 149°04' east, with the mainsail reefed, and the No. 2 Genoa furled as the French yachtswoman was sailing to windward. *Ecureuil* fell into a bigger than usual wave, and in the strong shock the mainmast was broken at the first spreaders. Isabelle was hand-steering at the time. 'But,' she said, 'in the dark I could not see the waves.'

Then, on Christmas Eve, Philippe led in a group of seven finishers in some twenty hours. His time was 29 days, 15 hrs, 32 mins, 8 secs. He was not pleased. He said he had built a boat to race in 50-knot winds. There had been very few 50-knot winds and the boat would 'be ready tomorrow' to begin the next leg, he said. He was clearly very disappointed at what, barring major problems for the three ahead on the succeeding two legs to Newport, seemed certain to be the end of Philippe's splendid reign as BOC 'king'.

Philippe's disappointment could not diminish, though, the remarkable conclusion to the voyage from Cape Town that brought seven skippers across the line over Christmas Eve and Christmas morning. The seven, in order of finishing, were Philippe, David Adams, who had fought so staunchly with the demanding *Innkeeper*, Mike Plant, Kanga Birtles, Jose de Ugarte, Bertie Reed and Yves Dupasquier. That, with the exception of the disabled *Ecureuil*, which finished shortly before 3 p.m. local time on 27 December, was the conclusion of the 'first division' contest – which by general consensus included *Servant IV*, the Class II winner for the second successive stage.

Left   David Adams' *Innkeeper* under sail from Sydney to Punta del Este

Right Yukoh Tada entertained many dockside crowds with his spontaneous
jazz concerts, conducted in his customary ebullient style

6   Unfailing Heroes

Josh Hall got into short-handed racing by accident. A serious knee injury playing rugby football forced him to give up contact sports and to abandon hopes of a naval career. So at eighteen he had set off for two years of hitchhiking around America, South America and Europe. When he returned to England he had no job and not much idea of what he would do. When a friend who was a foreman for the construction of Robin Knox Johnston's 60-foot catamaran *British Airways* asked Josh if he wanted a job, he was quick to accept – though, he says, he made in jest what was to be a momentous proviso. 'I said "Yes" to the job,' he says. "But only if it includes taking the boat for a sail in Harwich Harbour.' Well, the sail around Harwich Harbour turned into three years with Robin, the best apprenticeship anyone could have. It introduced me to a sailing world I never knew existed.'

Once Josh decided to do the race he set out to get more relevant experience, which was to include competing in the single-handed transatlantic race of 1988 and winning his class in the 1989 Round Britain race. In the transatlantic event he sailed his former, 34-foot *Spirit of Ipswich* – also named for his home town and local sponsors – but raced the new *Spirit*, Mike Plant's old boat, in the Round Britain event.

'I bought *Airco* in London, without even inspecting it,' says Josh. 'She was the right pedigree, the right boat to buy. From the outset I wanted a boat that was designed and built for single-handing.'

For three years before the race, he says he 'lived and breathed The BOC Challenge.' And, like so many of the skippers doing the race on the shoestring – in all three classes – his dedication to the project was to remain undiminished whatever the adversity.

Altogether, *New Spirit of Ipswich* suffered five knockdowns on the Cape Town–Sydney stretch, and it was during the first that Josh dislocated his right knee, the one he had hurt playing rugby; the one that got him into singlehanding. When he got to Sydney he was to learn that he would have to have an immediate operation to remove a cartilage, and then, when he got back to England, it would be necessary to have a second operation to 'rebuild' his knee.

It was not the end of Josh's problems. Three-quarters of the way to Cape Horn on the subsequent stage three, he suffered a knockdown with *New Spirit of Ipswich* that essentially destroyed his boom and maybe his chances of being in the first three in Class II in Newport.

'It was my only knockdown of the third leg. The boat was coping really well. Sure it was uncomfortable, but it was safe. The winds were about 60 knots and I was down to just a storm staysail. But it was not the wind that did the damage; it was a mountainous wave. It flattened '*Spirit*', driving her mast into the sea, and bent the boom to about 60°.'

Engaged in a tough tussle with *Project* and *Buttercup* (*Sponsor Wanted*, before Don secured sponsorship with one of Australia's largest bakeries, after arrival at Sydney) since Sydney, Josh was very upset about the time he might lose. But the first priority was to 'splint' the damage; before the boom broke in two. The two ends were kept together only by the small section of unbroken aluminium on the inside of the bend.

After rounding Cape Horn, Josh accepted a Chilean Navy escort to Herschel Island, in the Woolaston Chain behind Cape Horn, where he anchored to carry out further repairs. He had the help of Chilean navy ratings which meant that he was able to enjoy a five-hour sleep, a shower and a meal. Altogether he was halted for some nineteen hours.

Robert Hooke did not complete the second stage of the BOC voyage until 5 February, two days after the main fleet had departed Sydney on the third leg. *Niihau 4*, Robert's Ron Holland-designed, Dekiri-built 45-foot, fibreglass cutter, was named after an island at the end of the Hawaiian chain. Altogether, he had been delayed for some twenty days by collision repairs and the stepping of a new mast to replace the one damaged in the Southern Ocean.

Robert hoped to repair a troublesome automatic pilot and deal with faulty wind instruments and set off on the third stage within a couple of days. It was not to be. It was not until 11 February, eight days into the race, that Robert was able to rejoin the fray. He had been towed out to the start line the previous day, and then towed back when it was discovered that his wind instruments were still not functioning correctly. Then, he encountered a rigging problem that proved too great to permit him to continue without further repairs. He decided to withdraw.

Hal Roth, the oldest and one of the most experienced offshore skippers in the race, was also a late starter from Sydney after his enforced return to Cape Town for repairs. His time for the second stage was 67 days, 8 hrs, 53 mins, 37 secs. His total time for the voyage at that stage had been 122 days, 6 hrs, 33 mins, 46 secs.

Hal, who completed the second stage on 31 January, restarted on 7 February. It was a plucky decision; not unexpected of *Sebago*'s skipper. But he was to continue to plough a solitary course. Hal had gone to some length to make his yacht more competitive than in the 1986–87 race. He was out of luck from the start, however, and the story of his trials and tribulations is likely to be one this great author – often acerbic and unforgiving – will one day tell himself.

Another story of disappointment, of not being right at the forefront of the fleet, is the one that can be told by Nandor Fa, who finished the second stage on 16 January. His time, in view of his return to Port Elizabeth, was some 53 days. Nandor believed that, had he not had to go back to Port Elizabeth, he might have finished fourth in Sydney, ahead of Jeantot. *Alba Regia* completed the voyage from Port Elizabeth in 27 days, 20 hrs. He estimates that from Cape Town he would have taken between 26–28 hours longer. 'Of course,' he acknowledged in his ready way, 'I had different winds. But I'm disappointed at

Right New Spirit of Ipswich restarts from Sydney. The yacht was sponsored by some thirty businesses in Josh Hall's home town

the outcome. Still,' he added, as agreeably optimistic as ever, 'it is very nice to think about the next race.'

The saddest story of all was to be that concerning Yukoh Tada, a hero of the first voyage, whose hopes and ambitions for the third race were to end in Sydney after a multitude of vicissitudes.

It was a sequence from the film *High Society* at the Newport Jazz Festival, showing a yacht under sail as pianist Thelonius Monk performed, that led Yukoh to decide that he should buy a boat. He saw the film nine times before, sixteen years later, he arrived in Newport to compete in The BOC Challenge 1982–83. Tada had plenty of adventures in that first Challenge, going as far as 62° south to sail the shortest distance to Cape Horn on the Sydney–Rio de Janeiro stage. He was the third to round the Horn, his southerly route having paid off handsomely.

It was a far less happy story for Yukoh in the 1990–91 voyage. Yukoh had a difficult opening stage from Newport, but it was the second stage, during which he suffered very badly in a tender yacht, that led to his decision to withdraw. 'The race was much harder than my last one as I was knocked down much more,' remarked Tada-san after his arrival in Sydney – the 18th finisher in 51 days, 13 hrs, 35 mins, 49 secs.

'I was knocked down five times. One time I was almost capsized in 60-knot winds and huge waves. The weather conditions were pretty much the same as in the last race (1982–83), but my boat is faster this time and easier to capsize.'

He did not restart with the fleet, and it was confirmed on 15 February, some twelve days after his fellow skippers had sailed from Sydney, that Yukoh had decided not to continue. In a statement, the Tada-san camp explained: 'He was extremely exhausted with the second leg, and his back, injured in a traffic accident several years ago, started to ache. As the doctor has diagnosed that Yukoh is not in a state to continue the race, he has regrettably decided to retire.'

The decision saddened the huge numbers of friends and supporters Tada-san had gained around the world; they were to be further saddened with the devastating news, which came as the yachts were finishing in Punta, that Yukoh had taken his life.

In the words of the official BOC statement: 'He was loved by all who knew him. He was one of the finest examples of the human spirit, sensitive to the needs of others, and with an immensely generous heart. With Yukoh's death, everyone involved in The BOC Challenge had lost a great friend.'

During the race, however, the BOC 'community' found another Japanese friend in Minoru Saito, who impressed everyone with his enthusiasm for the voyage. He arrived ahead of Yukoh in Sydney, having offered to go to the assistance of the Japanese skipper he held in such awe after the troubles mounted aboard *Koden VIII*.

Minoru was as cheerful as ever when he completed the second stage, but as he complained, 'It was too cold and too rough. Because of the movement of the yacht I have much mess below. And it is too rough to use the heater.' But Minoru, who says he spent twenty-seven years 'working almost every day without any holiday', was very happy that he was now doing what he wanted to do: 'Sailing and not working.'

He was to develop two mottoes to help bring him through adversity: 'Come Hell come high water,' was one. 'The other,' he said, 'is bullshit the waves.' He shouted the abuse at the waves each morning, he says, because he so disliked the rough weather.

Saito-san suffered a multitude of problems and adventures that included *Shutendohji* being laid flat or knocked down about twenty times. Minoru had also suffered a broken forestay and halyards; lost his spinnaker pole over the side; had four of his sails badly torn, and lost power so that he could not use his auto-pilots, his radio or cook for ten days. His wind generator failed less than two weeks out of Cape Town. He was also worried that his centreboard might have broken.

Jack Boye was very clear in his condemnation of the second leg. 'It was a bloody awful trip. I never got into the race. The boat broke less than ten days from Cape Town and after that it was just a question of reaching Sydney.' His problems included the loss of his headstay, detached spreaders and the loss of all of his halyards.

Sad also, and a massive disappointment to the skipper, was the enforced withdrawal on the third stage of Robert Hooke. It was damage sustained in a collision with a trawler just short of the Sydney stopover that was to lead to Robert's eventual decision to withdraw, but like others the yachtsman had suffered one tiresome annoyance after another all the way from the Newport start to his retirement point in the Tasman Sea on his way to Punta.

Right   *Generali Concorde*. Some seventy per cent of the finishers
throughout the race arrived at night

7   *Icefields of the Deep South*

After two relatively tame stages, the third, most feared passage to Cape Horn and beyond of The BOC Challenge, was to provide more than enough savagery for most of the twenty skippers who embarked upon it.

It began quietly enough, with untypical calms in the usually ferocious Tasman Sea, and Alain Gautier took the lead he was to hold throughout the 7,200 miles to Punta del Este from just thirty minutes after the 3 February start off Sydney Heads.

Jack Boye's *Project City Kids* was first across the line during a problem-free, outstandingly spectacular start, but with David Adams carving a 400-yard lead as he drove *Innkeeper* on the southernmost course of the eighteen starters – *Sebago, Niihau 4* and *Koden VIII* were absent – towards the South Head.

Six hours into the race, there was a familiar order at the front: *Generali, Groupe Sceta, Credit Agricole IV* and *Ecureuil Poitou-Charentes*.

The early humour, Australian fashion, was provided by Kanga Birtles reporting that he had left his sea boots ashore. 'I forgot them because I never use them,' explained Kanga. 'I always sail barefooted. I even did the Round Australia Race barefooted.'

As the fleet settled down to a daily routine, it was variously suggested that Kanga put his feet in his pocket; that he 'glass them in', and, so as not to contravene race rules, Jose Ugarte recommended Kanga be provided with boots on medical grounds. Mike Plant's idea for getting around the rules was that a message be written on the boots. A written message and medical supplies are about the only forms of outside assistance permitted by the rules.

It transpired that there were no boots big enough for Kanga, whose use of plastic bags over socks inside a pair of shoes someone had left aboard – 'I wasn't going to ruin mine,' said Kanga – was so effective that it was to be imitated by more than one other skipper.

On 5 February, two days into the race, Christophe reported from *Groupe Sceta* that he had been in collision with a whale. Christophe, asleep at the time of the crash, woke up with his face on the deck, but reported that there was no damage and that he was proceeding serenely in sunny weather. The order then was *Generali, Groupe Sceta, Ecureuil, Allied Bank, Credit Agricole, Alba Regia* and *Jarkan*.

Two days later the first real storm, with 65-knot winds, settled the race fate of at least one competitor, Philippe Jeantot, who suffered a serious knock-down with *Credit Agricole*. Alain's *Generali* was knocked down, too, at 49°07′ south 166°25′ east, but escaped without appreciable damage.

Philippe, however, had to contend with a broken gooseneck and a badly torn mainsail. It was the first of a series of accidents to the winner of the first two BOC voyages, and led to Philippe branding stage three of the third BOC the worst he had experienced. He had never been more glad to finish a voyage, he was to say.

At the same time, the gooseneck fitting broke on *Project City Kids*, resulting in skipper Jack Boye being hit on the head by the boom. He agreed to call race headquarters every four hours until he was sure he had not been badly hurt.

After six days, Alain led Christophe by a mere twenty-five miles. On the seventh, Paul Thackaberry said he was headed for Bluff, New Zealand, to replenish lost diesel supplies on *Volcano*, and the Class II leader, *Servant IV*, had collided with a whale and sustained some damage to her false, collapsible bow.

By Day 12, Alain was at 61°39′ south, 145°56′ west, but still only ninety-four miles ahead of Christophe. John Martin was third with *Allied Bank*, which was some 157 miles back. And it was now that both John and Isabelle Autissier reported encounters with icebergs. Both skippers were around 60° south.

Isabelle reported her sighting through the ham radio net in New Zealand; John reported direct that he had encountered 'five huge icebergs and four growlers' – about 1½ miles apart and about one mile from *Allied Bank*.

'This was the most incredible sight I've ever experienced in my racing career,' he said. 'While very majestic to behold, at the same time they were awesomely frightening.'

John automatically dropped his spinnaker and altered course, and it was some three hours later, after some tense manoeuvring, that he was clear of the danger.

The following day, Nandor, deepest south with *Alba Regia*, saw nine icebergs at 63° south. As the Hungarian, on a heading of 130°, was sailing even deeper south, there were eight other yachts past 60° south and four more at 58 and 59° south. Most seem to have spotted icebergs.

In The BOC Challenge 1986–87 only Philippe Jeantot went to 62° south on the third leg, and only he and Jean-Yves Terlain, with *UAP*, went below 60° south.

Alain, only sixty-one miles clear of Christophe, was relaying the positions of the icebergs he saw to the skippers astern. He had altered course slightly north as first Christophe and then Philippe reported icebergs astern of him.

David Adams expressed his attitude very explicitly from *Innkeeper*: 'It's bloody cold and hard on the nose, with icebergs galore. I passed two this morning. I was within a mile of them and there are nine ahead of me. *Generali Concorde* has told us all their positions and I'm following his course.'

'Being fairly inexperienced,' he said when referring to the icebergs, 'I went quite close to them at first, to see what they were like. When I saw how many growlers there were I couldn't get far enough away from them.

'I saw quite a few, but the visibility was so bad that it was more usual to see them on the radar.

'My sole priority on this leg was to finish 4 days ahead of Kanga. I could not afford to go up north if I was to achieve that aim.'

He had started the voyage hoping to finish in the first three. It was his string of misfortunes on the first leg that led him to modify his ambition to being the first Australian at the Newport finish.

'At night I would sleep by the chart table. I always take half-hour catnaps. I have a half-hour alarm. I never sleep through it. I try to sleep where it is uncomfortable so that I don't fall into a deep sleep. I always sleep below and pop up top every half-hour. I've never slept more than four hours in a day since the start.

'I was just watching the radar. You know you're not seeing everything. You just switch off that part of the brain that might worry about icebergs. You become fatalistic. It was only that one time that I hit a growler. I always tried to give them a 2–3 mile berth.

'When we first got down to the icebergs, this is when I thought "this is where it starts to get serious". We're not playing any more. This is where the people with the nerves come out on top.

'From the common sense point of view there should be some control – like having to pass a point at 55° south. But I wouldn't want there to be a limit as to how far south you can go. Next time the bergs may be at 55° south and not at 63° south.'

Discussing the same viewpoint, Nandor also felt there should be no limit. 'I met a lot of ice,' he said. 'You can't avoid ice. In this race you just have to get used to sailing with ice. The risk is what makes the BOC the ultimate challenge.

'Without the dangers, without being tired, there is no risk and no displeasure. There is only pleasure if there is displeasure. I would go south for anybody else. Even to 70° south. But I don't know what to tell the others,' he confessed when the subject of rescuing a fellow skipper was raised.

'If you impose limits it just becomes an ordinary race, like Whitbread. It will kill the spirit of the BOC. The danger makes it fascinating. If someone wants to impose a limit of 60°, in a few years they will have reason to make it 55°.'

He said that his purpose in going as far south as he had in this race was twofold: 'To learn and because I needed to find the wind.' He continued: 'The ice was very frightening. Sometimes I had more than a dozen icebergs on the radar screen at one time. Once I had an iceberg on the screen and it disappeared at two miles. It was poor visibility. I saw it from on deck right in front of me at thirty metres. I tacked away to starboard and was very lucky not to hit it.

'Another time I came on deck and found I was in an ice field. The boat was being steered by the auto-pilot. I was in a channel without ice, but just clear for about two metres either side of the boat. It was a miracle I was where I was. It was nothing to do with me.

'Whether I would go south in the next race would depend on the weather, of course. I would like a router. I would be happier if there were no routers for anyone, but if everyone has a router, I must have one. Anyway, I will know much more about the winds.

'The south made me tired but it was not so scary as I would have imagined. It depends on luck. It does need a lot of energy to check the boat. But the farther south I got, the better I got to know where the growlers would be. After a while I know where the water is free of ice and where there will be ice. From my radar I knew which side to pass.

'I saw nothing smaller than 4-feet square. And much bigger. I even saw a collapsed iceberg. Generally the pieces were the size of half a house and up to three miles long.

'But my expectation was that it would be much worse,' remarked Nandor, recalling his earlier circumnavigation in a 31-footer. 'In the 31-footer in a big storm, it was very dangerous a lot of the time. It surprised me how much faster, how much more stable and how much safer the 60-footer was. ·

The Southern Ocean legs provided the most testing weather with winds in
excess of 70 knots

Children visiting Jack Boye's yacht signed his sails – he was sailing to raise money for a children's charity

Ecureuil   Poitou-Charentes'   broken
mast in Sydney. The mishap dropped
her to eleventh place

Isabelle Autissier celebrates her arrival
in Newport

Ecureuil Poitou-Charentes arrives in Sydney at the end of the second leg

Alain Gautier arrived in Newport 2½ days after Christophe Auguin. He described it as 'the hardest 48 hours of my life'

Generali's main sail in tatters at the finish in Newport

Class II winner Yves Dupasquier collects his prize from Dick Giordano, Chairman of The BOC Group

A triumphant Christophe Auguin on arrival in Newport

Groupe Sceta was modified for the conditions of the Atlantic and the Southern Oceans

Right *Servant IV* the most radical yacht in the race, was the only winner of all four stages

Volcano in Sydney – winner of the Corinthian class

Paul Thackaberry receives the special IBM Corinthian
prize from Jim Reilly – General Manager, Marketing
Services and Communications

Robin Davie and Don McIntyre with their awards for
'Best Communicators'

Christophe Auguin. Winner of The BOC Challenge 1990–91

'In the 31-footer I never met 70-knot winds. With the 60-footer I had 60 knots on the nose. I had to drop the sails. But the boat was remarkably stable, remarkably safe. I always felt very safe. This experience was interesting in a positive way,' he added.

While on Day 13 the leading boats were facing the iceberg hazard, Paul Thackaberry had been in collision with a whale, damaging the bow rudder of *Volcano* and causing a slight leak.

At this stage, Alain Gautier led by 61 miles from *Groupe Sceta*, 144 from *Innkeeper*, and 163 from *Allied Bank*.

The next day, 17 February, icebergs in large numbers continued to be the main worry of the leading skippers. Nandor, deepest south at 63° 20′ with *Alba Regia*, had seen fifteen; David Adams, at 62°12′ south, reported thirty.

David hit a couple of small ones; Alain was also in collision with a small growler and broke a secondary rudder. The icebergs seemed to be worse at around 62° south, the course being followed by *Generali* and *Innkeeper*, where visibility was down to two hundred yards.

It was that night of 17 February that John Martin reported he had been in collision with a growler, that *Allied Bank* was badly damaged, and that he was heading for southern Chile.

So there began close radio contact between the skippers at sea, and a long vigil ashore, that was to culminate in another classic BOC rescue in the Southern Ocean.

In a link through Sydney Radio, John explained that the main stringer had been broken in *Allied Bank*, which had also suffered some delamination by the keelson. John said the yacht was shipping water, though not badly.

The collision occurred at 60°30′ south, 129°38′ west, some 1,795 miles from Punta Arenas, north of Cape Horn. At the time of his collision, John had 50-knot winds. He dropped his sails and headed north under bare poles to find calmer waters. His new heading meant *Allied Bank* was on a converging course with the approaching *Jarkan Yacht Builders*, *BBV Expo '92*, *Grinaker* and *Servant IV*.

Alain, meanwhile, was at 63°20′, farthest south of the fleet and some 114 miles ahead of *Groupe Sceta*. *Innkeeper* was 242 miles back, and Mike Plant's *Duracell* 320 miles behind *Concorde*.

On 19 February, as John Martin was proceeding somewhat anxiously north with *Allied Bank*, Robert Hooke announced his withdrawal.

Being battered by 35-knot winds on the nose, John had been forced again to reduce sail as *Allied Bank* began flexing in the rough conditions and showed signs of breaking up and foundering.

John's position, monitored steadfastly by all of the skippers on their four-hourly radio scheds and by those with GPS, was precarious. For although at least three skippers astern were ready to go to his assistance at a moment's notice, they were likely to be from four to six hours away at best – far too long if John had to be in the water in his liferaft in water at little above zero degrees for any length of time.

According to the skippers monitoring the unwelcome drama, the most powerful yacht in the race was breaking up in conditions that were threatening to deteriorate seriously very quickly. Storm force winds were approaching John's area of 59°47′ south, 124°34′ west.

John was fairly calm throughout, but clearly growing increasingly anxious as his situation worsened, and it was obvious he was much relieved once he had made the decision to abandon *Allied Bank*.

'He had just two options as far as I could see,' said Kanga Birtles. 'He could get on to *Grinaker* or go all out for Chile on a course similar to *Grinaker*'s to try to save *Allied Bank*. The second option meant he would run the risk that Bertie might be less close if *Allied Bank* did break up.

'To hear the statement, "I am surrounded by ice" usually indicated that people were very perturbed. When you see ice it has a very profound effect.

'My first sighting was of a berg that was three times as big as Lion Island, in Pittwater. It's a big lump of ice. You are sailing along and there is nothing there and suddenly there is this ice. That's when I first opened my rum bottle.'

Describing the collision and then his rescue, John, who had been alarmed by the closeness of a growler on the second leg, said he had decided not to go closer to icebergs than two miles.

'I was making 11–11½ knots in an east, nor'easterly when I saw an iceberg maybe three miles in length,' he explained.

'It was four miles distant. I was up on top putting in a third reef when the boat fell off a wave on to a growler. The damage was in front of the mast. The main structural beam, running fore and aft, was broken in two places – as though it had been sawn in half.

'I stabilized the problem and ran off without sails for twelve hours in 55-knot winds. Some twenty-four hours after the collision, there was no wind and flat seas. I tried to brace the boat and thought I would be able to get to Punta del Este.

'But then the conditions deteriorated again, and I had to go north-westerly for one day at 7½ knots without sails to try to keep the boat together. When the winds got up to 65 knots the boat began to delaminate.

'From the time I first spoke with Bertie until I was aboard *Grinaker* took about eight hours. There was exceptional camaraderie. It makes it safe for us to sail. The problem I encountered could have happened just as well with a crewed yacht. The BOC is still a great challenge. No one should be too worried about the accident.'

When John decided to abandon *Allied Bank*, he was 58°07′ south, 126°17′ west. After the skippers' 'chat hour' on 20 February, the day of the rescue, Bertie Reed, closest to the damaged craft, was reported headed for *Allied Bank*.

The wind was then around 65 knots, and the conditions were described as 'horrendous'. Weather reports indicated there was a very serious depression in the Southern Ocean, centred on 57° south, 130° west. The low registered 938 millibars.

It was at 13.16 GMT that Sydney Radio reported Bertie was preparing to take John aboard and it was finally reported through Portishead Radio at 15.35 GMT that John had safely made the transfer.

Bertie explained that 'John is fine,' and that the rescue had been 'a very traumatic experience'. He expected the stricken vessel, fitted with a keel of spent uranium, to founder 'within 24 hours'. John had effectively scuttled the great yacht before he abandoned her; *Grinaker* was some 1,958 miles west of Cape Horn.

John, who donned a wet suit for the transfer, explained that the winds had abated to between 35–40 knots when Bertie got to him. 'We had spoken on the radio for six hours,' he said. 'I put the liferaft in the sea with some provisions and clothes and equipment in it and tied on a long rope. I then got into the liferaft and planned to throw a line to *Grinaker* and cut the line to *Allied Bank*. The line to *Allied Bank* broke.

'I was about a half mile astern of *Allied Bank* when Bertie arrived and circled the boat looking for me. We made the connection the second time Bertie circled me. There was about a foot of water in the liferaft. The water temperature was 4°.

It was two days later before John began to feel properly warm. He had been in the liferaft less than thirty minutes. Said John when it was all over: 'I shall be coming back to do the race again.'

8   *The Going Gets Tougher*

Briton Robin Davie at the wheel of his 40-foot *Global Exposure*,
the oldest and smallest boat in the race

While John Martin was being rescued, Alain Gautier, still deep into ice territory, was more than doubling his lead over Christophe Auguin in second place.

'Having got to 64° south, I tried to avoid the very low depression that was a problem for all of the boats behind me,' explained Alain. 'Before the depression I had a lead of 150 miles. It quickly became 300 miles.

'But the worst problem was the icebergs. I counted forty and then stopped counting. During fifteen days the only work I did was avoiding icebergs by radar. It was very poor visibility. I didn't see the sun for two weeks.'

With *Generali* constructed of aluminium, the conditions inside the yacht were 'severe humidity and severe cold.' Alain explained that these conditions were 'very tough. It was very tough also for my nerves, and my nerves were not helped by some days of very light winds.'

His pattern in the Southern Ocean was to study the radar screen and sleep for one hour. 'I was doing 10 knots, the radar worked very well and tells me if there is any ice in the next 12 miles. So after an hour I wake up and return to check the radar.

'When I sleep or steer I like to listen to the boat. I listen to all the noises in the boat. After a time you know which are the good noises and which are the bad noises.'

Generali's skipper, who went only to 59° south and saw no more than a dozen icebergs in the Globe Challenge, said the weather was the real reason he went so far south in The BOC Challenge. 'I had no choice,' he commented. 'It was the only way to go because that was where the wind was.' And he rejected the idea that he had made the decision because of advice from his router in France. He said that talking with his router before the start was more important than regular contact during the race. 'I'm not sure that routing is all that important,' he mused. 'But working before the race with the router and spending a long time about all the routes is very important.

'It is interesting that so far in this race, after three stages, that the route I have taken is very close to the one we had chosen in advance. For instance, we decided on 61° as the best latitude to cross from Sydney to Cape Horn.'

Alain also commented on the demands of steering a large yacht like *Generali Concorde*.

'You have to think a lot,' he says. 'Before you do anything you have to think what you have to do and prepare the tasks in an order to do them. I think about what I have to do and analyse what has to be done. I steer mostly with the auto-pilot and computer. When I'm sailing upwind I use the auto-pilot twenty-four hours out of twenty-four hours. Downwind, in more than 30 knots, I steer. On this leg I use the spinnaker a lot, so in this case I steer for up to eighteen hours a day. When I have just the Genoa and the main I steer only when I think I can gain some extra miles.'

On 20 February, when John was picked up, Alain, at 64°24′ south, 102°37′ west and within 2,500 miles of Punta del Este, led Christophe by 340 miles. The order, with distances behind Alain at that time was: *Groupe Sceta*, 343 miles; *Innkeeper*, 400; *Credit Agricole IV*, 403; *Duracell*, 462; *Alba Regia*, 499; *Jarkan*, 675; *Ecureuil*, 694; *BBV Expo '92*, 703; *Grinaker*, 790; *Servant IV*, 793; *Project City Kids*, 1,099; *Buttercup*, 1,207; *New Spirit of Ipswich*, 1,254; *Volcano*, 1,513; *Shutendohji II*, 1,622; *Global Exposure*, 1,646; *Sebago*, 2,744.

Philippe, meanwhile, had also been in collision with a growler. No damage was done to *Credit*, but Philippe had to endure the alarming experience of having a block of ice jammed between the rudders for three to four hours.

On 21 February, Day 18 of the Sydney–Punta stage, the storm was now centred on 57° south, 122° west and still a major menace to most of the fleet. The ARGOS pictures on race headquarters' IBM computer-screens were perhaps the most riveting of the race, showing as they did the violent changes of course made by almost all in the vicinity of the storm to avoid its fierceness.

It was a particularly worrying time for race officials, manning the race office on a 24-hour basis to keep close watch on developments in the fleet as the storm was raging, and compounded by concern over the safety of Christophe Auguin and *Groupe Sceta*.

In 40-knot winds, Christophe's ARGOS beacon was washed overboard, and he was later to report problems with his mainsail, ballast and telex. One of his ballast tanks flooded the main cabin, causing major havoc below, and a very tired Christophe was unaware that his ARGOS beacon was missing until told so by his French base.

The time it took to establish that the 'very peculiar behaviour' plotted for *Groupe Sceta* was in fact a rogue ARGOS beacon, floating in the opposite direction to that of her former parent yacht, was one of grave concern for race officials. It wasn't possible to contact *Groupe Sceta* to establish whether Christophe was aboard or injured, and there was concern lest incautious questions would raise unnecessary alarm.

When it was finally established that Christophe was safe but did not know he had lost his ARGOS beacon, the spare beacon – carried by each yacht in the third BOC Challenge – did not work when it was 'switched on' aboard *Sceta*. From then until Punta del Este, Christophe had to report his position daily by radio. It meant there was always thereafter some uncertainty about who was second in the fleet.

Alain, meanwhile, with a 353-mile lead, was essentially becalmed in an occlusion between two weather fronts at 65°14′ south, 98°15′ west. 'It was my worst day. I made only eighty miles in twenty-four hours.'

Day 19, and the weather conditions continued to concern race officials, though the depression, now registering 958 millibars, was moving very slowly and was less intense.

Nandor Fa, at 61°04′ south, 113°43′ west, was meanwhile reporting 75-knot winds, and Alain was now 400 plus miles clear of anyone. Next day all but *Alba Regia* and *Generali Concorde* were north of 60° south, and all were making between 9–11 knots as they endeavoured to reduce Alain's lead.

The next day was poor also for the leader, who progressed a mere ninety-seven miles towards Cape Horn when *Generali* was down to 2.8 knots. As there was conjecture that Alain, still at 62°15' south, might continue to struggle against less favourable conditions than skippers farther north, David Adams reported that the inner forestay had ripped out of *Innkeeper*'s deck, that a solar panel had been lost in the steep seas, and that he had had to repair a torn headsail. Discussing the conditions during the storm, David remarked that 'there were a couple of times when it was touch and go; pretty awesome stuff.'

His compatriot, Kanga Birtles, had suffered a bad knockdown, with the mast of *Jarkan* in the water. The masthead instruments, VHF radio aerial, video camera and stanchions were broken or lost over the side, and *Jarkan*'s large spinnaker and No. 1 headsail were badly torn.

Below deck he was clearing up hamburgers in the forecabin that were lost from the freezer aft. Kanga also expressed his frustration at having lost so much distance because of going too far north because of the iceberg hazard.

'The mast went under the waves to an angle of about 45°; the keel was 45° up into the air. I was on the underside of the coach roof. It was pretty scary.'

Kanga said his main alarm had been the water temperature. 'It was cold; very cold. It made me realize how vulnerable I would be if water in any quantity got into the boat.'

At around the same time, the third Australian, Don McIntyre, suffered two knockdowns and a 360° rollover with *Buttercup*. He described the experience as 'like being in a tumble-drier.'

During Day 20, Alain made better progress, covering some 177 miles. The following morning he was making 12.1 knots, he still led by 154 miles and he was within 500 miles of Cape Horn. At the same time, Jack Boye, at 57° south, became the first of the Class II or Corinthian skippers to report ice.

On 26 February, *Generali* had closed to within 275 miles of Cape Horn, but was making only 5.4 knots at 59°19' south, 72°56' west. Alain was to round safely at 0.400 GMT the following day and he headed for the Strait of La Maire, between Tierra del Fuego and Staten Island. *Generali* was making 14 knots.

During the next few days, ten yachts were to round Cape Horn, with the greatest number ever, seven, rounding on 2 March. The seven, who followed *Groupe Sceta*, *Innkeeper* and *Duracell* were *Alba Regia*, *Servant IV*, *Credit Agricole IV*, *Ecureuil Poitou-Charentes*, *Grinaker*, *BBV Expo '92* and *Jarkan Yacht Builders*. There was less than 150 miles between first and last of the seven; there was only 67 miles between second and the seventh.

The order at Cape Horn, and the times of rounding, were: *Generali Concorde*, 07.50 GMT, 27 Feb; *Groupe Sceta*, 11.15, 28 Feb; *Innkeeper*, 14.00, 28 Feb; *Duracell*, 21.00, 28 Feb.

Mike said the weather conditions were identical to those when he rounded four years ago: 'light winds and flat seas. I wished for more wind, but I was still very excited … mesmerized … by the Horn. It was beautiful, very majestic. I never get tired of rounding it.'

As the seven skippers were rounding Cape Horn, and John Martin was being taken off *Grinaker* by a Chilean naval vessel, Paul Thackaberry suffered a deep facial cut as a consequence of being hit by the mainsheet during a gybe, and Alain, within 740 miles of Punta del Este, was making close to 9 knots.

Once round the Horn, Bertie Reed moved to fifth place, though there were only sixty miles between his *Grinaker* and Yves Dupasquier's *Servant IV*, in eleventh place. Right behind Bertie, Philippe's *Credit* and Kanga's *Jarkan* were equal sixth.

It was now known that Philippe was having to deal with all sorts of difficulties aboard *Credit*, which had lost part of her bow in the collision with the growler. Before that, there had been the broken gooseneck and the torn mainsail. Other setbacks included a leak, a burnt-out starter motor on the generator engine that prevented the use of all electrical and electronic equipment aboard, and damage to all but the storm jib of Philippe's sail inventory.

For Bertie and Philippe, the only two competing in their third successive BOC Challenge, it was a rare development. It had not been a happy voyage for Bertie, who had expressed his intention of quitting big-time solo sailing after the BOC, nor for Philippe who was having his worst voyage ever. But one thing Bertie could delight in was his position ahead of Philippe, practically the first time he had been so placed since he and his great adversary and friend first met in the first BOC in 1982–83.

Further back, there were two more roundings of Cape Horn, Don McIntyre in bright moonlight in a 30–45 knots of wind, and Jack Boye who suffered a knockdown in 60–70 knots of wind.

'It was absolutely incredible; crystal clear, lit by moonlight,' said Don. 'I sat in the cockpit for forty-five minutes just gazing at the Horn. For once I didn't have my camera on, because it was only moonlight.'

Jack was to report 'a shambles below' after *Project* had been knocked down five miles south of the Horn. 'It couldn't be better, though,' he was to say. 'After being knocked down off the Horn, whatever happens to me now will be just an anti-climax.'

At the back of the fleet on 5 March, Robin Davie was reporting that he expected to be in Punta around 22 March. He was still 2,000 plus miles from the finish; about 600 miles from Cape Horn, and he had trouble with his windvane, which he had dismantled and repaired. He'd earlier spent several hours up the mast repairing his radar detector. Around this time, *Generali Concorde* was just 122 miles from the finish.

It was on 6 March that Alain Gautier completed the third stage to the most tumultuous welcome of the race so far at 02.21.14 local time. *Generali* looked as smart at the finish as when she sailed from Sydney, the only hitch of an otherwise outstanding finish being that Alain missed one of the final marks of the course and lost some 40 minutes as he returned to rectify his mistake. Alain's time was 31 days, 3 hrs, 21 mins, 14 secs, giving *Generali* a total time for the three stages of 96 days, 10 hrs, 59 mins, 7 secs.

Clearly exhausted from his astonishing endeavours, Alain said the worst thing for him so far during the voyage 'was the last fifteen days on the third leg.'

He said there were 'pressures and pleasures' from being ahead. 'It is good for me psychologically and there was no big pressure in the early days of the leg because there was such a long way to go. But as time goes by the pressure builds. I work better when I'm ahead. When I'm ahead I'm very happy to be ahead. I do everything to stay ahead.'

It was some thirty-four hours after Alain had finished, at 12.39.42 local time on 7 March, that Christophe became the second finisher. David Adams and Mike Plant completed the third stage on 8 March. Mike was 6½ hours behind David, whose worst moment, he said, was being washed over the side on the end of his lifeline in a ferocious storm off the Falklands.

The next day, Robin Davie rounded Cape Horn, going to within a quarter of a mile of the promontory because the visibility was so poor. There was no way he was going to miss seeing the Horn, he said, though he confessed his action was not the best seamanship.

Right   Project City Kids approaches Sydney

THE THIRD TIME AROUND

On 10 March, Day 35, Bertie Reed was the first of the 'Magnificent Seven' to complete the third stage at 3.10 local time. He was just sixty-seven minutes ahead of Isabelle's *Ecureuil*. Jose and *BBV*, the favourites of the Uruguayans who had already become fanatical about The BOC Challenge, was next, followed in order by Nandor and Kanga. Nandor got ahead of Kanga only a few miles from the finish and the two skippers were just seventeen minutes apart across the line.

Philippe was the tenth finisher, his worst ever placing, and Yves crossed the Punta line, bathed in strong sunshine and with a stiff westerly breeze at 14.31.11 local.

A battle that had gone on since Sydney was finally settled in the Plate Estuary on the morning of 14 March, victory going to the American Jack Boye over the Australian Don McIntyre by some 2½ hours. The result earned Jack second place in Class II. Two days later, Josh Hall, with a broken boom and a 20-foot tear in the jib of *New Spirit of Ipswich*, still managed to beat Paul Thackaberry's *Volcano* into Punta.

It was on 18 March that Robin Davie sailed *Global Exposure* across the Punta line, and Minoru Saito became the seventeenth finisher on 22 March. Cape Horn, said Minoru, was his worst, and best, experience. 'I went round in 70-knot winds'. he said.

The hero of many of his fellow competitors said he had experienced six or seven severe storms, with winds around 50–60 knots, but that it was worst at Cape Horn. 'I began to go round the Horn with one storm jib; it became two storm jibs', joked the third Corinthian finisher as he was applauded by a large gathering of spectators and admirers.

One of them was Kanga Birtles who said: 'Doing the race from Sydney in a 60-footer is a lot easier than in a 50-footer. I did the stage in thirty-nine days. Minoru has tacked many more times and made sail changes for an extra twelve days in a much less comfortable boat. I take my hat off to him.'

Robin Davie, another admirer, was very circumspect, though, about the hardships of the skippers of the smaller yachts. 'It's not such a big deal; it's not as tough as all that,' he said. 'In many ways a 40-footer has got to be a lot easier. The sails are smaller and easier to handle and so long as the gear and equipment are set up correctly it's OK. But you need to be sure that everything is properly sorted out and working correctly.

'My boat is probably much wetter than most. I get more seas on board. But the biggest difficulty is the psychological one of coming to terms with being behind everyone else. You're at sea longer and you have more gales to put up with when everyone else is in harbour. You end up covered in bruises from for ever being bumped and banged into everything. It's a constant problem.

'You're on the move all the time, though I usually get six hours sleep a day – in half-hour, 45-minute naps. Sometimes I even sleep for eight or twelve hours if I'm very tired. There are often times when the best thing to do is to go to bed. But there is a difference. I'm sailing to get round the course. I realize that however much I race my boat I cannot catch those in front. The harder I push the more likely I am to end up gybing and broaching the boat and damaging the boat without making any more miles.

'My view would be very different if I had a 60-footer with the budget to replace everything I broke at each stopover and a gain in mileage for my effort. I have to try to use weather tactics to get my good times, without pushing the boat to breaking point.

'I play a cassette or radio for twenty-four hours every day. I change the tape about every twelve hours. This way I hear noises I like to hear rather than noises I would rather not hear. But the hatch is open all the time. I like the sounds outside. But I don't like slamming to windward; from wave to wave. At times I really wonder which will break first, the boat or me.

'But being becalmed is worse. There is usually a swell and the sails are flogging and the boom banging and it is tremendously difficult to get used to it', he added.

Hal Roth came home on the morning of 29 March, some 2 days, 16 hrs behind Minoru and the day before the rest of the fleet were to restart for Newport.

Right   Class II victor Yves Dupasquier in *Servant IV*. For much of the
race Yves was well up with the Class I boats

9   *The Tables Are Turned*

Punta del Este was a paradise. The welcome, the weather, the hosts and the ready friendships quickly forged were all genuinely cherished. After the frustrations of Sydney's Darling Harbour, which could not provide all the highly specialized facilities that round-the-world yachtsmen require; and the exhaustion and demands of the classic stage around Cape Horn; it was an ideal haven in which skippers could recuperate.

Despite some doubts that the halt would be too short for skippers to prepare for the final sprint to Newport, when the time came everyone professed to having their boats ready. A number were eloquent in their assertions that the yachts were better prepared than at any time previously.

Thirty days seemed to be the favourite total for the winning time for the final, 6,000-mile stage. It was about 1,000 miles longer than the previous final stage from Rio de Janeiro, for which the record winning time by John Martin and *Tuna Marine* was twenty-six days.

Alain Gautier, the race leader and favourite to win overall, said he was relying on the first-leg sails that took *Generali* to Cape Town in record time. Christophe Auguin said he had a huge new, 150-square-metre mainsail. Bertie Reed believed the final stage would take thirty-five days to complete; Philippe Jeantot declined 'making any more predictions.'

David Adams had lightened *Innkeeper* by about a fifth of a ton, by removing sails and equipment which included his dodger; Kanga Birtles had a new headsail and new spinnaker and believed the first yacht could be in Newport by 28 April. Don McIntyre, the third Australian, had 'no top secrets for this leg – I'm using my sails from Leg 1.'

Robin Davie: 'I just hope we get some good weather and some good sailing. I expect the final stage to take me about 43–45 days.

Paul Thackaberry: 'I want to be in Newport three days ahead of Robin. I've carried out all the repairs necessary. I'm in better shape than for the start of any of the previous stages.

'I'm now supported by *Innkeeper*, whose plywood dodger has been modified to provide reinforcement for the bow of *Volcano*.'

Jose de Ugarte: 'I've changed to a lighter No. 1 Genoa; I've repaired the main; all my electronics are now working; I've taken off the auxiliary rudders and I've removed the windvane.'

Nandor Fa: 'My purpose is to finish the race. The last leg should be good for *Alba Regia*, but I would love some new sails.'

Yves Dupasquier: 'I'm using the same Kevlar sails as for the first leg. I'm also taking some wine on *Servant IV* for this leg.'

Minoru Saito: 'All I have different is a new liferaft – to replace the one lost from *Shutendohji* on the last leg.'

It was all very friendly. There was no acrimony. Apparently no concerns or alarms. All eighteen skippers were heading off for what would include a Caribbean cruise.

But it was really war. Robin Davie was desperate to beat Paul Thackaberry, and vice versa; the rivalry was no less intense throughout Class II; the Adams– Birtles tussle in Class I to be top Oz was serious indeed, as was Mike Plant's desire to beat Philippe Jeantot. And Gautier was certainly concerned that Auguin might beat him, though he believed his advantage of '21.5 hours might be sufficient to win overall.'

As usual, though, Alain had Christophe at the forefront with him from the beginning, though the honour of being first across the start line went to *Buttercup* from *BBV Expo '92*, which later returned to Punta for Jose to replace a torn headsail.

Most impressive start in terms of good relations, however, was made by Robin Davie, who made a brief 'tour' of the pier to acknowledge with his klaxon the thousands of Uruguayans lining the shore to bid farewell to the single-handers they had grown to find enchanting.

On Day 2, as the leaders sped north-east, the three Corinthians, *Volcano*, *Global* and *Shutendohji*, were trying to get back into the race after lying becalmed for several hours right after the start. Once they got going, there seemed to be good sailing for the entire fleet, though skippers reported a number of close encounters with commercial shipping. Simultaneously, five yachts, *Generali*, *Sceta*, *Alba Regia*, *Credit* and *Innkeeper* were battling for supremacy at the front.

It was on 2 April, three days after the departure of the seventeen other competitors, that Hal Roth put to sea; and two days later, with the yachts cracking along, ARGOS was already predicting that Christophe, now the leader by a narrow margin, could be in Newport by 25 April with an unthinkable twenty-six-day passage.

The leaders continued virtually unhindered, but the tailenders were slowed by a high. It was to be a feature of the race, which at this early stage still had Nandor Fa's *Alba* in fourth place behind *Generali*, *Sceta* and *Credit*. *Alba* had been in collision with an unknown object, believed to have been a container, while Isabelle's *Ecureuil Poitou-Charentes*, at fourteen knots, had notched the top speed of the final stage.

Robin Davie radioed the next day that 'everyone is enjoying the sailing if not their positions.' He was alluding to the discomfort of Thackaberry, forty miles astern. But Paul was going to have to get used to it as Robin steadily built upon his advantage all the way to Newport.

The order was already settled in Class II as well, with *Servant* leading from *Buttercup*, *New Spirit of Ipswich* and *Project City Kids*. It was to be a simple leg for Yves, who encountered little trouble throughout and relieved his boredom by playing a big selection of tapes daily – including a special choice for the first skippers' chat hour of the day.

The events at sea became almost as predictable as Yves' daily disc; there were three races: *Sceta*, *Generali* and *Credit* had their event at the front; the rest of Class I had their battles; and it was the usual 'fare' at the back. The weather was just as predictable: the three leaders had it all their own way – until the Bermuda high – while the rest had less steady conditions but still reported excellent sailing.

The mystery was provided by Christophe, who from Punta had doubted that Alain's 21.5-hour advantage would win him the $100,000 first prize: because, it seems, he had successfully fooled everyone into believing he represented no real threat. He had set out to do just that; before the race began, during the race, and certainly, so far as Alain was concerned, all the time he was in Punta. It was his main intention, he says, to give the impression that there was 'no need to worry about Christophe.' All through the race, Christophe's objective was to show that he did not represent serious competition. 'You don't have to worry about Christophe,' was what he wanted the other skippers to believe.

He never tried, he says, to be the first through the middle section of the BOC. He didn't want four months of stress by being at the front round the world. He preferred to put the stress on Alain.

'I don't manage the race the same way as Alain, who wants to go fast,' says Christophe. 'The only thing was that I didn't want to be more than 100 miles behind. I am managing the whole race. I have no stress; I'm cool.'

Not so Alain: he knew the last leg would be tactical. 'It would', he declared, 'be a long match race to Newport.' He acknowledged that he and Christophe had been very close for much of the time since the start of the race. But for the last stage he was happy to be starting with a 21-hour advantage.

'But we will be passing through some very difficult areas like the Doldrums, and then we have the Bermuda high,' he said. 'It is not an easy leg. The conditions should be easier. But tactically it will not be so simple, because I have to cover Christophe. I will try to stay with him, but sometimes I shall have to take my own decision and go my own way.'

It was to be a much tougher proposition than that; Christophe had done far more planning for victory in the BOC than was appreciated.

'We planned the BOC victory from the drawing board,' he says. 'When we met to consider the design, and looked at the pilot charts, we concluded that the BOC was a race that could be won in light winds. We built the boat for light winds.

'The idea is to win the BOC in the Atlantic; in the south we are content simply not to lose. So I was not worried about the 21.5 hours. I still know it is possible to win; when we reach Punta we're back in the Atlantic.'

He says that the big mainsail was considered before the race began. Twin backstays were provided for this possibility. 'But I wanted to "taste" the boat before we made the decision about the big main. In fact, I telexed my decision to have the sail after I departed Sydney. I have tasted the boat. A solution is in my pocket. For this boat and for me, the big sail is a very good decision.

'But the last leg is a new situation for Alain. In the earlier legs when he decides to accelerate I don't go with him. In the last leg when he accelerates I go with him. It is not possible for him to go in front. He is used to going ahead and then controlling the race.'

Christophe developed his skills through the classic sailing system, starting with dinghies, 420s and 470s, which he raced between the ages of thirteen and sixteen. His father, who was a sports teacher, was his first instructor; Philippe Poupon, one of the truly great French offshore skippers, was another; and he got a lot of advice and learned a lot from Lionel Pean, skipper of L'Esprit d'Equipe, the Whitbread Race handicap winner.

Offshore, his first experience was cruising with his parents, and then, living in Granville, competing in all of the main Royal Ocean Racing Club events. In the 1979

Groupe Sceta's winning margin over *Generali Concorde* was just 2½ days

Fastnet Disaster he was sailing the Nicholson Half Tonner *Beep Beep*, caught in the worst of the storm in the Western Approaches and forced to retire to Milford Haven with a broken mast and badly damaged coach roof. Christophe was twenty at the time, the boat was very small, and he remembers the experience very well. 'I see the same seas in this BOC, for sure,' he says, 'but for a maximum of perhaps two hours. In the '79 Fastnet the conditions last for twenty hours.'

He has done five Figaros, the most important of all French 'proving grounds'. Everyone who is anyone in ocean racing competes in the Figaros. Christophe won at his third attempt, in 1986. He won two of the three legs in achieving this triumph.

He remembers well the advice he got from Lionel Pean before his first. 'The message, about "managing a race," is "not to accelerate all the time but to accelerate only when it is important to do so" ', says Christophe. He is a very serious sailor.

Just as serious is the deep rivalry that exists between Christophe and Alain. In five Figaros, Christophe has been ahead in just two. In the last two Figaros he had an old boat while Alain had a new one. But Alain has won only one Figaro in ten attempts.

The psychological effect of his actions on Alain was an integral part of Christophe's last-leg strategy. ' "If I do this," I say, "is it good for the weather, is it good for Alain?"

'If I have two options that are nearly equal I take the solution that is most likely to disturb Alain. On the final leg I never spoke to Alain. I never speak to any skippers.

'Alain has no confirmation of whether I am happy or fatigued. But one sentence by him was very important. It came in a television interview. In answer to a question, after we had come through the Doldrums, Alain says: "Christophe is 70 miles ahead. It is not a problem, I am going to overtake him."

'This is when I say to myself: "Alain is not going to do it." And this comment is good for me because I believe I know Alain is worried and it helps me to reassert my determination to win.

'What do I say when I am asked about the lead? "Oh, the race is not finished; it is possible to win; we are sure of nothing." I know my boat. I know in Punta that my boat is ready.'

Christophe says he was first to transform his boat for the conditions in the Southern Ocean. That was in Cape Town, after the first, Atlantic leg. In turn, Christophe was first in Punta to modify the boat for the return to the Atlantic. 'In a future BOC, I would go so far as to change the mast and the keel,' he says, paying special tribute to the staff he needed to do the work. This included his parents, both teachers, who retired just months before the BOC to accompany their sailor son throughout the voyage.

Alain began to wonder whether he would win the day before he crossed the Doldrums.

'I didn't stay close enough to Christophe on the Brazilian coast. Christophe went closer; to within twenty miles. He has more wind the day after we leave the Brazilian coast. During this one afternoon he takes twenty miles off me. He arrives at the Doldrums thirty miles ahead. That was the start of the end. Before that, during ten days I stay with him. I had the same speed.'

Alain saw Christophe's new mainsail as only a 'very small plus'; more a psychological advantage to Christophe. And Alain insists that he knew in Punta that it was too soon to consider himself the race winner.

'I know I can break the mast, for instance,' he says. 'After you have sailed around the world the boat is tired. We check everything; but we can't check everything. I know I will only win when I am at the finishing line.'

He knew that Christophe was a very good sailor; he knew that his rival had a very good boat; he knew that the skipper of *Groupe Sceta* would do everything he could and take every chance to win. 'But twenty-one hours is a nice cushion,' said Alain.

He did say before the start, however, that for him, 'the most important thing is to be ahead of Christophe.'

Recalling that on the second leg from Cape Town he had come from a hundred miles behind to win, he still considered the 'best solution' would be to stay close to Christophe.

He was later to say that on the last leg, after the Doldrums, the favourable trade winds had meant he could sail only a straight course to Newport and he did not have the opportunity to cover his rival.

'On the way to Bermuda there were no problems so far as equipment was concerned. Nothing important broke. But it is tough. Every day I work on board. There is not a lot of time. It is a little more exhausting day by day. As we approached Bermuda I knew the end would be difficult.

'Then, when Christophe crossed the finish line I was 175 miles out. I was making between 10–12 knots. Two hours later I was stopped with no wind.'

Alain says that when he departed from Newport at the start of the race he thought it would be good to finish in the first three. It was only after the first leg that he thought victory would be possible.

He scores his performance on the first leg 17/20. The second he scores 13/20: 'I was upset because of a difference of opinion with my router. On the second leg, I wanted to take the course that John Martin followed. I was persuaded not to.'

He scores himself 19/20 on the third leg but only 15/20 on the final leg. 'I know my race and I know every mistake I make', he says. Perhaps his biggest misjudgment was underestimating Christophe.

'My only mistake', says Christophe, 'is on the third leg, when I allowed Alain to escape to more than 100 miles ahead of me.'

It was when the skippers were dealing with the deep depression on the way to Cape Horn that he made his mistake. Then, when Alain went south, Christophe went north, so that the depression lay between the skippers. 'I was very angry', says Christophe, 'when there is 300 miles difference between us at Cape Horn.'

He was the more angry because of the 'calculated risks' he had taken to stay with *Generali* during the 'ice stage.'

He tried, he says, to go to weather of the icebergs to be clear of the growlers in their wake. But he went on the 'safe' side of the icebergs only when he had to. When he had ten or fifteen icebergs on his radar screen at the same time he would often go to leeward and the more dangerous side of the icebergs rather than make a major detour.

'I just hope these icebergs do not have any growlers in tow. Sometimes I am in icefields. I hear the noise, of the ice hitting the boat. It's like the noise of Scotch on the rocks. It's very special.'

On this Sydney-Punta stage, Christophe scored his performance just 11/20. This is because he believes his one mistake comprised two big errors: the first before Cape Horn, when he lost distance, and the second after Cape Horn when he made the 'mistake' of going outside the Le Maire Strait.

'But the last leg of BOC was the first on which I did not have any problems with the boat; the first when nothing broke. My luck, a very important part of sailing, had changed.'

Beginning Day 11, as *Generali* and *Sceta* closed to within thirty-six hours of the Equator, Nandor began to fade. The unfortunate Hungarian, so short of funds and suitable equipment for a very fast boat, was to be the final Class I finisher in Newport, some nine days behind the winner.

Christophe crossed the Equator at 00.32 on 11 April. He led *Generali* by sixty-three miles; he was 3,000 miles from Newport; he was still expected by 25 April – three days earlier than suggested by even the most optimistic of predictions.

Christophe made what was to be his winning move on 9 April. Alain was on the coast of Brazil heading for the Caribbean Sea. Christophe was to seaward of him. Alain came off the coast believing Christophe to be to the east of him. Christophe had gone inside and when Alain altered course to the west it was too late. Christophe had gone. He had found thermic winds which did not materialize for Alain further offshore.

Does he have a special talent for reading the weather? His answer is that from the age of fifteen he had begun to ask why the same people continued to beat him to win races. 'I decided', he says, 'that it is partly because they have a better knowledge of the weather. So I try to learn about the weather.'

Christophe paid particular attention to the weather prospects for the final leg of the race to Newport. 'It turned out to be everything I thought it would be,' he says.

As *Sceta, Generali* and *Credit* crossed the Equator and sliced through the Doldrums, they were to find north-east trade winds that remained with them for upwards of nine days, ensuring a rapid progress, and predictions by ARGOS by Day 14 of the race that Christophe would win on 24 April by sixteen hours.

Normally, Christophe sleeps 'according to the weather.' He knows his needs and sleeps maybe two or three hours. In the Doldrums, the first crucial part of the voyage, he had no sleep for forty-eight hours.

In the Trades he would sleep for a total of eight hours a day; sometimes even ten hours. 'When I arrive off Bermuda I am in very good form', he asserted.

Alain feels that Christophe took a 'calculated gamble' in the Bermuda high. 'According to my charts there is no wind,' says Alain. 'I go more westerly and there is no wind. In this one day I don't know how Christophe can go so fast.'

According to the *Generali* skipper, it is taking this 'risk,' this 'calculated gamble,' that earned Christophe what was to become the real winning lead. It is what Alain calls a 'unique solution'.

He argued that Christophe appreciated there was no risk to his second place because Philippe was too far back in third place. And it was now that the penalty, the 16.5 hours, came back into Alain's mind.

'I would prefer it, when we reach Bermuda, that I am thirty-eight hours ahead. I wonder, in this case if he will take the same "calculated gamble." '

Christophe was much more positive about the situation. 'I know there is a chance to win when I depart Punta. On my mind is the fact that we design for victory on the drawing board.' He clearly did not agree with Alain's summation that 'the race is won and lost in the last 200 miles.'

According to Christophe, he recognized that the Bermuda high was going east from the cloud formation, though the forecasts had indicated after he arrived off Bermuda that no wind would arrive from the west for two to three days.

'At this time it is very important to win in latitude,' Christophe explained. 'What is the speed of the high in the west direction? I need to know. I see there is movement from the clouds. I'm at the limit of the clouds.

'When I see the position of the high from the clouds, when the clouds go east I go after them. I follow the clouds along the anti-cyclone. I take the autodromic way. Meanwhile,

Alain is going west for security. I have a lead of 150 miles. For him this is very dangerous.'

Indeed, it was fatal. The story, as Alain explains, ended with him running into a 'hole' two hours after Christophe crossed the finish line at 1-11-22 on the morning of 23 April. *Groupe Sceta* had completed the final stage of the race in a remarkable 23 days, 13 hrs, 39 mins, 42 secs – nearly three days faster than it had taken John Martin to complete the 1,000-mile shorter leg from Rio four years previously.

Christophe's time around the world was just 22 hrs, 36 mins, and 35 secs over the 120-day mark, and the time was a staggering 13 days, 4 hrs, 46 mins, 30 secs faster than Philippe's winning time in 1987.

It was not until some two and a half days later that Alain completed the course, his last lap taking 26 days, 1 hr, 50 mins, 10 secs.

'As I wait for the wind to go in pursuit of Christophe, I think many times about the Figaro race that I lose when I become becalmed three miles from the finish,' says Alain. 'I think about it when I enter the Doldrums. I think I had lost one race this way and I hope it is the last. But it is not to be.'

Word came from sea when it was confirmed that Christophe had won that Alain was 'very pleased for Christophe.' Says Alain: 'I'm very disappointed, of course. But that's life.' In fact he was devastated. 'It's an experience; a big experience,' he says. 'It was the hardest forty-eight hours of my life.'

Right   *Groupe Sceta*, Newport

10   On Reflection

The other outstanding saga of what was generally a fairly straightforward and uneventful final stage, centred on the outcome of the Corinthian division. The arrival of Robin Davie in Newport on 9 May, some six days behind Christophe, and at a point when Paul Thackaberry was still becalmed 500 miles out, meant that there was an outside chance *Global Exposure* rather than *Volcano* would emerge as the Corinthian champion.

Robin's fourth-stage time was 39 days, 21 hrs, 49 mins, 42 secs, giving a total for his circumnavigation of 181 days, 18 hrs, 17 mins, 17 secs.

Before the start from Punta, *Global Exposure* had trailed *Volcano* by 4 days, 16 hrs, 58 mins, 56 secs. The question was whether the American skipper could hold on to the advantage he had gained by being the first Corinthian finisher in Cape Town, Sydney and Punta. It was to become a close-run thing, for when Paul finished in mid-afternoon on 12 May his lead over *Global Exposure* had fallen to less than one-and-a-half days.

Last back in Newport, Paul's slender advantage was sufficient to secure for him the $30,000 Corinthian Class prize and the $10,000 that went with the special IBM Corinthian award. Christophe's victory had secured $100,000; Yves Dupasquier, the easy victor of Class II, won $30,000; and in all three classes the runner-up won $20,000, and each of the third-place finishers $10,000.

Paul was in high good spirits when he completed the race, though his progress had been affected more than that of any other skipper by frustrating calms. Similar conditions had ruined Alain Gautier's hopes of victory and had upset the late ambitions of a number of skippers – most notably Jose de Ugarte, Nandor Fa and Jack Boye. Generally however, as the record times emphasize, competitors were delighted with the conditions between Punta and Newport.

The comment by Robin Davie, on 8 April, just a week into the deciding sector of the voyage that, 'everyone is enjoying the sailing even if some are not enjoying their positions', pretty much summed up the position. 'It's very reasonable here at the back of the fleet,' he said. 'It's been a most unusual air flow. We've had following winds all the way from Punta.'

Two days later, Bertie Reed expressed similar sentiments: 'It's been a very simple trip. It's unbelievable. Eight years ago we were doing 120 miles a day. Now we're doing 300 miles a day. Normally on this leg you get light, following breezes. We have had north-easterlies for most of the time.' On 15 April, Philippe Jeantot was to say, 'The sailing conditions are absolutely ideal.'

Philippe was to finish some thirteen hours after Alain at 2:34:38 on the morning of 26 April, coming third was a further French triumph in a race dominated since its inception by yachtsmen from France. He confirmed later that The BOC Challenge 1990–91 was to be his last solo yacht race. 'There are other things in life', he said. 'I have not lost my enthusiasm for sailing; I am not going into the mountains to escape from the sea. But I have had my last race. I wanted to win, but the race was a pleasure for me even though I did not win.'

Philippe believed that it might still have been possible for him to have won the third BOC had he done especially well on the third stage from Sydney to Punta del Este. 'But I knew when I arrived in Punta, after the worst stage for me in all three BOC races, that I could not catch Christophe or Alain. On the final leg I wanted only to regain third place. To do this, I had to recover four hours that I had lost to Mike Plant and *Duracell*. On the last leg I was 140 miles ahead of Mike, by more than four hours, after just four or five days. I was very lucky with the Doldrums. For me they lasted just overnight.

'And right on the Equator, I picked up the north-east trade winds that remained with me for nine days. For those nine days I was never below 11 knots. My best day's run was 295 miles. I had an average speed of better than 12 knots.'

It was close to two-and-a-half days after Philippe had completed the race that David Adams, one of the new ocean-racing 'giants' to emerge from the BOC, crossed the finish line. Then, as if to further emphasize the close fought nature of the competition, within the next forty-two hours there arrived, in order, Mike Plant, Isabelle Autissier, Jose de Ugarte, Kanga Birtles, Bertie Reed and Yves Dupasquier. Mike moved up to fourth place overall, followed by Kanga, David, Isabelle, Bertie, Jose and Yves.

One of the elder statesmen of the sport by virtue of his three circumnavigations in five years, Mike Plant had started the race with the stated ambition of winning the race, and an undisguised belief that he had the boat and the ability to do so. He considered his fourth place, hard-earned though it was, no consolation.

Mike had stated before the restart from Punta that there would be no room for mistakes if he was to hang on to the slim advantage he held over Philippe before beginning the last leg; and though he was displeased by the margin of 3 days, 5 hours the great French yachtsman had built over *Duracell* on the way to Newport, it was clearly the lead of nearly twelve days that Christophe had gained during the race that most disappointed America's fastest round-the-world solo sailor.

Naturally taciturn, Mike found it difficult to discuss his performance publicly, and he could not disguise the deep disappointment he felt at having lost. Deep down, he probably knew as early as Cape Town that to achieve his ambition of winning the BOC he would need a lot of luck during the subsequent three stages if he was to make up the vital time he had lost on the first stage.

At the end he preferred to consider the future, and the possibility of competing with a new and improved yacht in the second Globe Challenge, less than two-and-a-half years away at the end of the third BOC. He believed he had learned what was needed in the last race just ended, he said, to succeed in the next Globe.

Kanga and David, fifth and sixth on cumulative times behind Mike, had in effect completed two races when they returned to Newport: the BOC, and the race within the BOC to be the top Australian. It was a gentlemanly 'contest' won by the droll, sage Kanga against the shy, sharp David. Kanga's *Jarkan*, sixth on the opening leg, finished ahead of David's *Innkeeper* only in Cape Town, but consistency throughout meant that the advantage of 4 days, 15 hours built on the first, Atlantic stage was defended with such certainty that Kanga achieved overall victory over David by some seven hours. David had been forty-seven hours behind when he sailed from Punta.

Kanga was pleased, too, at being first to complete the course without the advantage either of a Kevlar mainsail or a router. Like his Class I compatriot, he was quick to acknowledge the advantage the French yachts ahead of him had in design. Kanga, who sailed a sound, thoughtful race, had the advantage, unlike David, of competing with the yacht he had specially built for himself. He suffered no major equipment failure throughout what for him was to be a 30,000-mile race. Kanga also raced to Torquay in the inaugural BOC Transatlantic Challenge that followed the race round the world from Newport to Newport.

The factors that distinguished David were his outstanding racing ability, and his determination to succeed with a less-than-ideal yacht that was only rivalled by Robin Davie down in the Corinthian division. David had seemed well out of the race when he arrived ninth in Cape Town, but he was to outdo himself on the succeeding three stages with a yacht built to IOR (International Offshore Rule) to be raced by a large crew.

'If David Adams and Robin Davie had boats like us,' remarked Alain Gautier after the finish of the race, 'it might have been an Australian or British win instead of one for France.' But when it comes to discussing 'what if', there is no more fascinating question about the race than what might have been but for the dismasting of Isabelle's *Ecureuil Poitou-Charentes* on the second leg. For as events proved, Isabelle concealed a wickedly competitive determination beneath her gentle manner, and won the unreserved admiration of all single-handers.

'I'm the same', said Isabelle, when asked to talk about any effects the race might have had on her. And it is the certainty that she is the same, in terms of her happy, friendly disposition, that has made her so endearing to her fellow circumnavigators. In terms of sailing, the little-known Isabelle with an uncertain pedigree who started from Newport, completed the voyage as yet another undisputed French yachting 'giant'. Leg after leg, Isabelle demonstrated that she is a formidable skipper, who seems certain to challenge the very best in the sport in succeeding races if she starts with a really competitive vessel.

Isabelle had cause to be sad about her final placing, but with perhaps less reason than Bertie Reed who finished behind her on a voyage for which he hoped that he had at last found a winning boat. Apart from the third stage, on which he finished fifth, the race was not a happy one for Bertie, who frequently expressed disappointment at *Grinaker's* failure to perform well downwind.

Bertie avoided giving explanations about what he said would be his final solo voyage, but was evidently disappointed that he did not complete his farewell to sailing with greater distinction. 'I've made a lot of friends around the world during these BOC races,' he said. 'I always enjoy returning to Newport. It's been wonderful. This last BOC has been a sort of cruise around the world. Rescuing John was nothing. A guy calls you up on the radio and tells you he wants you to rescue him and you do it.'

A veteran of three BOC races, Bertie's expert seamanship, cunning and natural ability are undisputed. In the first BOC in which Philippe Jeantot's superiority was so overwhelming, Bertie was by far the best of the also-rans. However, like so many of his peers of those earlier single-handed days, there is now doubt whether he possesses the super-sharp racing edge that is today demanded of those who would win marathon ocean voyages. What was an adventure has now become a grand prix race.

The development brings no discredit to the natural ability of Bertie and his fellow sailors in so many other areas of ocean-racing from the Admiral's Cup to the Route du Rhum. Not only have you got to have the best boat, equipment and the best back-up, but you have to possess also the very best yacht-racing talents.

During the race Bertie built a great friendship with Jose de Ugarte. Their prolonged daily discussions during the skippers' chat hour became a popular feature of the race. Jose, one of the true gentlemen of the sport, nearly quit the race in Cape Town so disappointed was he with his performance. He thought that he had a good competitive boat, and had hoped to finish well up the order. Jose was exhausted when he reached Cape Town after a voyage frustrated by a series of equipment failures and adverse weather conditions. His comment, which he offered when he reached Newport, that he had 'drifted all the way here from Punta del Este', was typical of the remarks about the weather made by 'Captain Sunshine', as he became known to his fellow skippers.

'I didn't like the first leg and the last leg', said Jose on his return. 'I don't like "coastal" sailing. I've been pretty happy doing the single-handed transatlantic race. I like that. I wouldn't mind doing the two Southern Ocean legs of the BOC again. I would enjoy that. But I would not enjoy the two Atlantic legs. The wind was too light too often for me.'

Yves Dupasquier, the Class II winner, who was both tenth to finish and tenth in the overall placings, was even more outspoken: 'I'm a bit fed up with sailing', he said. 'I want to go away and do something different.

'I wouldn't want to do the race in a 60-footer; it's too difficult. I am basically lazy. That's why I sail the 50-footer.'

Yves, an intellectual, had indicated that if he ever did consider doing the BOC again it would be in a 50-footer rather than a 60-footer because of the lower costs and easier handling involved. He indicated that he would make sure that his next 50-footer, if she was ever built, would go to weather – perhaps the one deficiency of *Servant IV*. On the other hand, Yves also stated that he didn't like going to weather, so when *Servant* slowed on the windward stretches it may have been the disenchantment of the skipper for the conditions that had something to do with the performance of the yacht.

Nevertheless, the showing of Yves and *Servant IV* in The BOC Challenge 1990–91 was a genuinely great effort. Apart from the first stage, when Yves confesses to having gone the 'wrong way', the 50-footer was always racing with the 60-footers, and often ahead of several of them. It was perhaps surprising that the only 60-footer that *Servant* finished ahead of was the disabled *Alba Regia*. 'How could I finish ahead of Bertie and Jose', asked Yves when asked why the superiority of his yacht at sea had failed to be matched by her position in relation to the 60s?

Nandor Fa was to suffer more than his share of ill luck on the final stage. The forestay broke on *Alba*, and he slipped down the order in the calms off Brazil. He fell further behind in a succession of windless zones over the concluding miles from Bermuda to the finish. Some other skippers, who had noted the lack of sturdiness in much of the equipment with which the Hungarian began the race, also point to some inconsistency in his sailing – most notably the way he fell from the front of the fleet as the yachts were leaving the Doldrums. But it was there that Nandor complained of a back injury that might have had more to do with his performance than he was to admit.

Despite his many problems throughout the third BOC, and despite fading to fourteenth

Right Runner-up Alain Gautier receives his prize from Patrick Rich (*left*), Chief Executive, and Dick Giordano, Chairman of The BOC Group

in the overall order behind the trio of yachts, *Buttercup, New Spirit of Ipswich* and *Project City Kids*, which finished behind him at Newport, Nandor stamped a large, indelible mark on the legend of the BOC race. Here was an enormously popular skipper; enormously powerful, enormously intelligent, and one who fought with enormous determination. We may well hear more of him in other races – the Globe, or even the next BOC.

The next three finishers, Don McIntyre, Josh Hall and Jack Boye termed themselves the Three Musketeers. They were a jolly trio who seemed to enjoy themselves whatever the adversities. 'We realized early on that we could not catch Yves and *Servant IV*', said Don. 'And as the race developed there built up an incredible relationship between Josh, Jack and me. We had a classic race.'

Josh Hall explained that, 'We acted as our own weather analysts; we didn't have any routers. A great closeness developed between Don, Jack and me, a closeness born out of the rigours of the voyage. The support of Jack and Don when I dislocated my knee was immense.'

The Three Musketeers, in constant radio contact and in a race of their own for much of the way, as the 60-footers and Yves sped away in front and they outdistanced the following Corinthian class skippers, were notable for the way in which they reported their progress to shore support teams. Don stated before the start that for him there were two races, 'the BOC and the BOC media race', and in terms of media success in Australia he probably emerged as a winner in the media category. Josh Hall achieved much in this respect also, especially by his assiduous reporting for *The Times* and Anglia Television.

Don suffered his fair share of problems during the race, though in comparison it was a much, much tougher race for Josh and Jack. Josh was very stoical about his misfortunes: 'this race is all about fortune: you get 'breaks' with the weather, you get 'breaks' with the gear and it is as a consequence of the 'breaks' that you come out on top, or not. The lesson from the broken boom and the 19-hour stop at Cape Horn for repairs is 'never give up'. Anything can happen. Because despite all of my problems, I found when I got to Punta that I was still ahead of Jack. Instead of being right out of the race, I finished third in Class II.'

The race between the Aussie *Buttercup* and *New Spirit of Ipswich* was very close all the way, though the British skipper managed to finish ahead of his Australian rival only in Sydney. *Project* won the first stage, but was then to finish behind *Buttercup* and *Spirit* on all three of the succeeding stages.

The final stage of the race from Punta was largely trouble free for skippers, but on 27 April Don was to report that the stem fitting of the chain-plate on his *Buttercup* had pulled out. The mishap, which occurred in only 12 knots of breeze but an 8-foot swell, resulted in a 10-inch hole appearing in the bow. The outer forestay was also broken. Don reported that the number two forestay was the 'structural one' so the rig was not in jeopardy. But the accident took its toll, for Don finished only some eight hours ahead of Josh back in Newport, and a little more than three-and-a-half days clear in second place on the overall standings. Jack was less than half a day behind *Spirit* after 27,000 miles.

Jack, who suffered a series of crippling equipment failures, said that the voyage had made him realize 'how sweet and precious life is.' Noisily greeted by his former high school classmates holding a class of '61 reunion in Newport, Jack said that he had learned a lot during the voyage, and intended in future 'to take life less seriously and have lots more fun.' Complimentary about every aspect of The BOC Challenge 1990–91, Jack said: 'Comparing the Vietnam War and the Southern Ocean: Vietnam was safer.'

The fleet have named a section of the sea off Brazil after Jack Boye, whose *Project City Kids* was becalmed for two days. The area is now known to BOC skippers as 'Boye Bank'. For Don, who began with serious debts, the signing of a sponsorship deal in Sydney helped to lessen his financial worries. Josh found the race especially tough financially, and he had to find extra sponsors at every port of call to help meet his mounting costs. At the end of the race he stated that he had personal debts of some £24,000 with the company owning *Spirit* owing £120,000. Jack, however, could afford paid assistance at each stopover to help prepare his broken boat for further action.

After *Global Exposure* reached Newport on 9 May, the finishers were Hal Roth on 11 May and Minoru Saito and Paul Thackaberry on 12 May. Hal, last of the Class II competitors, had a total time of 211 days, 17 hrs, 12 mins, 43 secs. His time for the final stage, most straightforward of what for him was an otherwise troublesome voyage, was 39 days, 0 hrs, 21 mins, 1 sec. Hal had some seventy-two hours deducted under the rule that allows late finishers of the preceding stage to start the subsequent stage late without penalty. It was about the only 'break' he got in the loneliest of all the voyages in the third BOC. That Hal should have soldiered on, ploughing a solitary, unprotected, unescorted course around the bottom of the world, rounding Cape Horn for the third time, is one of the most remarkable achievements of the race.

Minoru Saito, undertaking his first circumnavigation, became one of the heroes of the 1990–91 race for which his total time was 197 days, 20hrs, 10 mins, 59 secs. He took 42 days, 21 hrs, 4 mins, 54 secs to reach Newport from Punta. Completion of the voyage was a great personal triumph for every skipper, but for none more than Minoru, who demonstrated exceptional fortitude in surviving countless crises and ordeals in a voyage that took some seventy-seven days more than the winner. Minoru never complained, his arrivals were always the most enthusiastic, and he won the unreserved admiration of his fellow skippers along the way for his pluckiness. After him came Paul Thackaberry to complete the Corinthian fleet.

In its way, the Corinthian triumph by Paul, the last of the main group to depart Newport and last to return, was no less remarkable than Minoru's. Because of pre-race problems with the boat he had designed and built himself, there were not a few on the Newport waterfront who doubted that Paul would complete the voyage. That he did so, dealing with a multitude of setbacks and annoyances, was an astonishing achievement, worthy of the great legend the BOC race has become.

There was no one more competitive in this group, or the entire fleet, than Robin Davie who surprised practically everyone he sailed with in the 1990–91 race with his determination and ability to perform so well with the 40-foot *Global Exposure*. Robin had lots of minor problems during the course of the contest, but they were never too big for him to come to terms with. No one worked harder to prepare his boat for each leg; no one worked longer or exhausted himself more in his tireless efforts to continue.

For all but the five skippers, Kanga, Bertie, Jose, Josh and Robin, who were to go on to compete with Warren Luhrs in The BOC Transatlantic Challenge, it was the end of the voyage. For many, though, it would probably be no more than the end of the beginning of a career in short-handed ocean-racing. For no fewer than eleven of the finishers, Christophe Auguin, Alain Gautier, Kanga Birtles, David Adams, Isabelle Autissier, Nandor Fa, Don McIntyre, Josh Hall, Paul Thackaberry, Robin Davie and Minoru Saito, expressed the hope that they would do the race again.

Christophe Auguin could become the new Philippe Jeantot of the BOC. He has the same, thorough, businesslike approach. Indeed, he came to the third BOC as an established businessman. He has a four-man, £450,000 company, Mer et Communication, which he set up in 1987–88 when, without a sponsor, he didn't race at all. He likes skiing and hang-gliding and has a licence to fly an Ultra-lite. But yacht-racing is his top priority, and after Newport he was preparing to compete in the great French La Baule-Dakar race.

What makes Christophe stand apart is his ability, like that of other top French skippers, to prioritize. 'I know that luck plays a big part in every race', he said in Newport. 'But it is possible to minimize the risks. And to do well the first priority is your race staff. The race is the second priority. I know I'm just 50 per cent of the effort. The other 50 per cent is the staff.'

It was a 'method' that ensured Christophe's great triumph, achieved with a remarkable average speed of 8.4 knots. Christophe's average on the first stage, when he sailed 6,693 nautical miles, was 7.39 knots. The average over 6,329 miles on the second stage was 7.31 knots. From Sydney to Punta, Christophe's average with *Groupe Sceta* was 9 knots for 6,853 miles, and on the way to Newport the average of the top combination was 9.95 knots over 5,636 miles.

Christophe says he would like to do one Globe Challenge – 'but not soon.' He is already planning for the next BOC Challenge in 1994–95.

Alain is naturally a little circumspect about the next BOC after the trauma of the last. 'The BOC 1990–91 is in the past. I have to forget it. Now I am thinking about another race; perhaps a multihull campaign. But for me each race is different. Will I do the next Globe? Will I do a multihull campaign? One can depend on the other. If I do a multihull campaign then it is unlikely I will do the next Globe. If there is no multihull campaign then I might do the Globe and after that it would depend on whether I win the Globe.

'But a multihull would be a great experience. And I think I will be back in the BOC in four years time. It is a great race.' Then again, he muses, 'four years is a long period. I think my life is on the sea. But it is possible even that I will change sports. Maybe I will take motor-racing more seriously.'

For the rest of those who have expressed the hope of doing the next race, ambitions seem certain to depend on sponsorship. Heading this list is Kanga Birtles, one of the most methodical of the skippers of 1990–91. Kanga wants to return with a boat that has got pace. 'Perhaps I might even be the pacemaker next time', he said. 'I shall go to a number of designers and see what they can offer.' After the race to Torquay, Kanga was hoping to sell *Jarkan*, though 'plan B' would have the boat in Plymouth and arrangements in hand to compete in the Royal Western's single-handed transatlantic race of 1992.

David Adams, forced by circumstances to sail *Innkeeper* back to Australia, was keener still to compete in the next BOC as part of a concentrated, prolonged short-handed campaign that would include the Figaro, probably the Globe and the single-handed transatlantic race, and then another BOC.

Isabelle Autissier, returning to France to a major civic reception, seemed as certain as any of the skippers to find the funds with which to contest the fourth BOC race, and it seems just as certain that she will do so with a state-of-the-art yacht that could put her in line to be the first woman to win the BOC.

Nandor Fa seems certain to obtain sponsorship from his native Hungary where he is a two-times national hero. Whether by way of the next Globe, with *Alba Regia* or with a new yacht, he will surely be back with a boat that could make him the first winner from outside of France. Whatever he might lack in technique, he is sure to make up for with determination and strength.

Don McIntyre, as good as any skipper from BOC 1990–91 at promoting himself, seems certain to find the sponsor to put up the money for a second, improved campaign; and it is just as sure, all things being equal, that Minoru Saito will be back – with *Shutendohji II* or a new, sponsored 50-footer. The only thing likely to stop Minoru is his health, though like everything else about his BOC, it seemed to get better and better the further he raced.

Josh Hall and Robin Davie, as eager as any to be there next time, hope to benefit not merely from their own exceptionally well-publicized, stoical efforts in the third race, but also from the race organizers' decision, stated after the finish of the third event, that the fourth BOC would finish in south-western Britain. Because of their records, they should be at the front of what could be a longer than ever queue of hopeful British singlehanders. The history of the BOC single-handed cause in Britain is a sad one; shown by the fact that Josh and Robin were only the second and third British skippers to complete the race. The first was Richard Broadhead.

Even before he left Newport Paul Thackaberry was preparing to build a new boat. He had the plans for his new boat before he reached Cape Town. As the voyage continued the plans were modified, and in Newport Paul enlisted the help of a professional designer to prepare a winning 50-footer for four years hence.

Paul was leaving for Oxford and home as the tiny transatlantic race fleet, headed by *Hunter's Child* (a boat that qualified but did not compete in The BOC Challenge), was leading the five other boats out to Rhode Island Sound from the Fort Adams start line.

The BOC Transatlantic Challenge was under different 'management' – sponsored by The BOC Group in association with Champagne Mumm, with the Magellan Systems Corporation providing the vessel position information, and Robin Knox-Johnston as race director.

Entry was open only to boats that had qualified for the single-handed round the world race, though the prizes of a purse of gold sovereigns for the first yacht across the finish line, and a similar award for the first on handicap based upon waterline length, could be won only by yachts that had completed the circumnavigation. Each yacht had to have a minimum of two crew, and although there was no upper limit, numbers were controlled by the amount of safety equipment aboard.

Jarkan Yacht Builders, the leading round-the-world contender, had as crew Richard Fryer and James C. (Jim) Reilly, General Manager, Marketing Services and Communications at IBM who had agreed his company's supporting sponsorship for The BOC Challenge.

Bertie Reed had as his co-skipper John Martin, with the yacht nominally renamed *Grinaker-Allied*, and the crew were Ret Goldswain and Jannie Reuvers.

On *BBV Expo '92*, the third round-the-world 60-footer to compete, Jose Ugarte had a crew of four: Ignacio Ugarte, a nephew, Ignacio Equiluz, who was the man responsible at the Bank of Bilbao for setting up Jose's sponsorship, Luis Guernos, who had been one of Jose's shore support team, and Dale Nelson, the Spanish skipper's host in Newport. There was considerable amusement as to how a crew of five proposed to live on a yacht that Jose had found cramped. Things would be very cosy with just Josh Hall and his brother Alan on *New Spirit of Ipswich*, and Robin Davie and his cousin Ian Heyworth aboard *Global Exposure*.

'Dark horse,' but expected to set the pace by virtue of starting fresh from Newport on what for the others was the final 3,000 miles of a 30,000-mile race, was *Hunter's Child*, skippered by Warren Luhrs. He had Nat Iyengar, Tim McKegney and Ian McKeckney as crew.

Crowds greet David Adams on his arrival at Newport

For all sorts of reasons, the west-to-east transatlantic contest had been considered but cancelled after the 1986–87 round-the-world voyage. There was considerable uncertainty about the transatlantic during the planning stages of 1990–91, but it was to prove a worthy forerunner to what seemed likely in future to mark the end of The BOC Challenge.

In covering close to 1,000 miles in the first three days and setting a 60-foot record mark of 344 miles during a 24-hour period, the performance of *Hunter's Child* was to prompt The BOC Group to put up two new prizes – a perpetual trophy for a record 24-hour run with a cretwed 60-footer, and another, similar award for a 24-hour record run by a 60-footer sailed solo in the round-the-world race.

Luhrs, who had decided after the two-handed transatlantic race of 1990 that he would not compete in The BOC Challenge 1990–91, was known to have a downwind flyer; and despite conditions that were anything but typical for the time of the year in the North Atlantic – north-easterly headwinds and more than two days of calms – completed the race to Torquay in 13 days, 10 hrs, 57 mins, 12 secs. It was a remarkable time when compared with those of vessels of more than 200 feet in times past, but Warren was 'disappointed.' He had been sure it was possible to complete the voyage in less than ten days, and the speed with which *Hunter's Child* had departed North American shores, leaving the round-the-world yachts in a foaming wake suggested then that a nine-day record was on the cards.

Hunter's Child was to make the headlines on both sides of the Atlantic again afater a collision with a shark, a strange coincidence because on her maiden voyage to America – she was built at Totnes, close to Torquay – the teeth of a shark were found embedded in her rudder after a similar collision in 1989.

BBV had actually been first to cross the line, the start signalled by the Newport Artillery Company, founded by George III and using a cannon that was cast by Paul Revere. And, *Hunter's Child* apart, there was soon the familiar close racing between the 60-footers. Bertie reported on the first morning at sea that he could see '*Jarkan* to weather' and *BBV* 'in the vicinity.'

Second day out, Robin Davie said it had taken *Global* an hour to pass a pod of whales travelling in a similar direction to the yacht, and then four days into the race he saw a second pod of perhaps 12–15 whales, 'probably hump-back.' He had also been slowed by netting caught in *Global*'s rudder and had been over the side to clear it.

Two days later, *Spirit* was in collision with a whale. 'It happened very quickly', radioed Josh. 'We were doing 12 knots at the time. We came to a grinding halt. I was in the bunk at the time and ended up on the deck. Alan, who was going up the hatch aft with a cup of tea, ended up in the forepeak with the cup but no tea.' Josh said it was the second time he had seen a whale during The BOC Transatlantic Challenge, and that he had observed more wildlife during the first days of the 'sprint' than throughout almost the whole of the round-the-world-race.

It was a week after the start from Newport that The BOC Group announced that the next BOC Challenge would end in Britain. Starting from the east coast of the United States in September 1994, the race would finish at a port in south-west England or south Wales in May 1995.

'We need a port that wants to participate in The BOC Challenge as an enthusiastic partner in the event', said Nigel Rowe. 'The race, and its associated education and environmental programmes, offer real opportunities for civic and public involvement.'

Moving the finish of the race to Britain would make the event more attractive to competitors and participating sponsors by adding another key market to the round-the-world course, he said. At the same time it was announced that the rules for the next race would include additions to enhance safety – relating to stability and seaworthiness – and to discourage competitors from venturing too deeply into the iceberg-strewn sections of the Southern Ocean.

The rule would come too late for John Martin, the next Torquay finisher aboard *Grinaker-Allied*. He and Bertie Reed finished at 6.18 local time on 5 June. Their time was 16 days, 0 hrs, 18 mins, 27 secs, some two-and-a-half days behind Luhrs. Starting with *Grinaker-Allied* there was then to be a rush of four finishers in eighteen hours. *Jarkan* was first at 11.11 p.m., *BBV* crossed at 5.46 on the morning of 6 June, and *New Spirit of Ipswich* completed the course at 12.37 p.m.

Grinaker won the purse of gold sovereigns as first 'official' finisher; *Global Exposure*'s arrival after 13.21 on 8 June meant that the handicap award went to *Spirit*. The transatlantic race was an interesting exercise, as a number of 'lessons' emerged regarding the proposed finish in Britain of the next BOC Challenge. First, there was the question of the finish, with skippers emphasizing the merits of a host port clear of channels or bays. Facilities were also uppermost in the minds of those who raced to England. As with the round-the-world event, there was little serious criticism, but a number of compliments for a well-run, well administered race. When the skippers met earlier in Newport to consider questions raised about the 27,000-mile event there had been near unanimous approval for the rules that had applied to The BOC Challenge 1990–91. Though BOC's Race Committee were naturally delighted at the 'vote of confidence', there was a quick reminder that it would not prevent changes if changes were deemed necessary.

What was especially interesting was the acceptance by the skippers that there was, indeed, a need for a time penalty. Some went so far as to suggest that the failure of a boat to arrive on time, perhaps two weeks before the next race start, should be immediately disqualified, except where there were acceptable, mitigating circumstances.

More surprising was the verdict that routers should be banned, and the emphasis that skippers would honour the introduction of any such rule. There was no support for the idea that the next BOC should be restricted to 60-footers only. Competitors felt that the existing rules governing size, stability and the use of exotic materials should remain unaltered; and it was similarly clear that skippers did not want any changes with regard to deck hatches or the time spent in the stop-over ports.

However, skippers did recommend a stricter adherence to a ban on advertising and no prize money for the Corinthian class; and they also asked for simpler qualification arrangements that would allow crews to help work up yachts during qualification voyages provided they were skippered by entrants who had competed in a previous BOC or Globe Challenge. While there was a belief that some limit should be placed on how far south yachts should be permitted to go, there was no unanimity on how this should be implemented.

Upon reflection, the skippers thought this race had been the best BOC of three. The boats, skippers and administration were better, and the interest generated in the race had been far in excess of that for the previous two races. There were faster times, better safety arrangements, fewer worries over the ability of skippers to take care of themselves – and the excellent development, inspired by the competitors, of a four-hourly chat-hour, had been responsible in large part for the no-nonsense rescue of John Martin by Bertie Reed.

The events surrounding the rescue were the only serious development to concern those ashore about those at sea throughout the race. The way in which the rescue was carried out largely without regular direct reference to the organization was of concern to race officials. It seemed that skippers in direct contact by means of sophisticated communications equipment with their shore bases, found it quicker and easier to pass on inter-fleet information this way than to communicate through race control. Race control still relies, of course, on the proven and reliable ham radio network that had provided a BOC race safety net since the inception of the event, and not on sophisticated communication equipment of the kind possessed by some competitors. No one regretted the upgrading of communications ability by the competitors; the lesson was for the race organization to be similarly equipped to monitor all inter-yacht communications.

It seems likely that the equipment of the better funded yachts in The BOC Challenge 1994–95 will be more advanced and demanding than ever. Race administration will have to keep well abreast of these changes. There will exist the means to interrogate special equipment aboard yachts to provide better and more detailed information about their position. It might not help communications to race control by skippers themselves, but it should mean that for the first time officials will be aware at all times of the whereabouts of the yachts.

Another message to come loud and clear from The BOC Challenge 1990–91 is that the renowned camaraderie of the skippers competing in the foremost single-handed round-the-world race has in no way diminished over the years. Even those skippers arriving late in port with slower or damaged boats were always a part of the BOC 'family'. It was an inspiration to see skippers of the faster finishing 60-footers arriving *en masse* in the early hours to greet a fellow competitor in even the most uninviting of conditions. And there were many instances when less fortunate competitors were taken under the wings of those with better financial or stronger numerical support. Furthermore, there were not a few boats that completed the race with equipment from rivals to tide them over because of shortage of funds or delivery problems.

The intensity of the competition among the middle-order 60-footers and in Class II, uniquely close for the ocean-racing event, in no way detracted from the splendid BOC 'standard' of looking out for others. When John Maratin was in peril, all around him endeavoured to offer advice, comfort and solace as he struggled in desolate wastes before calling upon his old shipmate Bertie Reed for rescue. John's emotional testimony in Punta to the power of the BOC camaraderie was one of the most moving experiences anyone in any BOC Challenge has experienced.

Winners of awards or merely winners (as all who complete this most demanding of all courses are known), those who comprised the third band of BOC skippers left no scars or bruises on this classic contest. All this despite the ever-mounting pressures that are the inevitable companions of tougher competition: the more demanding private sponsorship arrangements; the more acute attention to detail required by sophisticated equipment and more powerful craft; and the responsibilities and requirements inherent in stricter race rules and publicity standards. The contest's international importance is far beyond that even imagined by the competitors in the first such voyage.

If there is a conflict of interest in this great event, it is that generated as skippers try to meet their own needs while dealing with race and BOC Corporate 'needs': dealing with the day-to-day requirements of a campaign sponsor, while working on a boat, and also attending receptions mounted by a variety of voyage-related organizations.

'We feel we have to go to some of the more important receptions', commented one skipper. 'But it could be that it will cost several hours that are vital in the preparation of the boat for a subsequent stage.'

Quite clearly, there is also a potential conflict between what might be termed the 'duty' of The BOC Group to the race and the attendant needs of competitors' sponsors. As custodians of a 'maturing' race, The BOC Group faces an increasing multitude of demands that always come down to spending more money. It can be a formidable burden to a sponsor.

Some competitors, either generously supported by a major corporation or less well-endowed with cash from a variety of resources, sometimes believed that they had special needs that deserved exclusive or exceptional attention. There were even flagrant demands for what amounted to privileged status. Unhappily, the flow of assistance that emanated from the custodians was sometimes met by a steady ebb in performance from those assuming they deserved special treatment.

Skippers and supporters alike should be able to expect that the standards set in the management of The BOC Challenge 1990–91 will not slip. But they should take reassurance in the intention of The BOC Group to appoint an Event Manager to further improve the company's custodianship of a competition bound to face additional pressures as new stopovers are confirmed. If the result is a yet more professional approach it should bring added prestige and style to an event that promises to mature to greater perfection with even better boats and better skippers than the twenty-five that lined up off Fort Adams for what was to be The Third Time Around.

The BOC Challenge 1990–91 Records and Results

The BOC Challenge Records

1982–83	**Newport–Cape Town**			
Class I	Jeantot	*Credit Agricole*	47-00-01-02	
Class II	De Roux	*Skoiern II*	58-19-38-08	
1986–87				Improvement
Class I	Martin	*Tuna Marine*	42-01-10-36	04-22-50-26
Class II	De Roux	*Skoiern IV*	45-14-47-10	13-04-50-58
1990–91				
Class I	Gautier	*Generali Concorde*	37-11-12-39	03-13-57-57
Class II	Dupasquier	*Servant IV*	44-15-44-07	00-23-03-03
Corinthian	Thackaberry	*Volcano*	56-10-34-27	
1982-83	**Cape Town–Sydney**			
Class I	Jeantot	*Credit Agricole*	35-09-14-16	
Class II	De Roux	*Skoiern II*	46-01-30-08	
1986–87				
Class I	Lamazou	*Ecureuil*	28-07-13-22	07-02-00-54
Class II	Plant	*Airco Distributor*	34-16-03-52	11-09-26-16
1990–91				
Class I	Martin	*Allied Bank*	26-06-47-23	02-00-25-59
Class II	Dupasquier	*Servant IV*	30-12-02-13	04-04-01-59
Corinthian	Thackaberry	*Volcano*	38-06-49-20	

177

1982–83 Accumulative Times (Legs 1 & 2)

Class I	Jeantot	*Credit Agricole*	82-09-15-18	
Class II	De Roux	*Skoiern II*	104-21-08-16	

1986–87

Class I	Jeantot	*Credit Agr. III*	71-05-50-18	11-03-25-00
Class II	Plant	*Airco Distributor*	82-07-34-22	05-13-33-54

1990–91

Class I	**Martin**	*Allied Bank*	64-02-35-07	07-03-15-11
Class II	Dupasquier	*Servant IV*	75-03-46-20	07-03-48-02
Corinthian	Thackaberry	*Volcano*	94-17-23-47	

1990–91   Sydney–Punta del Este

Class I	Gautier	*Generali Concorde*	31-03-21-14
Class II	Dupasquier	*Servant IV*	35-15-32-11
Corinthian	Thackaberry	*Volcano*	41-10-04-52

1990-91   Accumulative Times (Legs 1, 2 & 3)

Class I	Gautier	*Generali Concorde*	96-10-59-07
Class II	Dupasquier	*Servant IV*	110-19-18-31
Corinthian	Thackaberry	*Volcano*	137-03-28-39

1982–83   Rio–Newport

Class I	Jeantot	*Credit Agricole*	28-17-11-35	
Class II	Konkolski	*Nike III*	32-11-13-20	

1986–87

Class I	Martin	*Tuna Marine*	26-00-50-20	02-16-21-15
Class II	Den Heede	*Let's Go*	27-04-40-20	05-06-33-00

1983–83   Accumulative Times (Legs 1, 2, 3 & 4)

Class I	Jeantot	*Credit Agricole*	159-02-26-01	
Class II	Tada	*Koden Okera*	207-13-55-45	

1986–87

Class I	Jeantot	*Credit Agr. III*	134-05-23-56	25-21-02-56
Class II	Plant	*Airco Distributor*	157-11-44-44	50-02-11-01

1990–91   Punta del Este–Newport

Class I	Auguin	*Groupe Sceta*	23-14-11-22
Class II	Dupasquier	*Servant IV*	30-20-30-56
Corinthian	Davie	*Global Exposure*	39-21-49-21

1990–91   Accumulative Times (Legs 1, 2, 3 & 4)

Class I	Auguin	*Groupe Sceta*	120-22-36-35	13-06-46-30
Class II	Dupasquier	*Servant IV*	141-15-49-27	15-19-46-30
Corinthian	Thackaberry	*Volcano*	180-07-39-42	

On This Day …

1990

Sept 21:	Enda O'Coineen back in Newport with dismasted *Kilcullen*.
Sept 22:	Bill Gilmore announces he is retiring.
Oct 4:	Don McIntyre in close encounter with freighter.
Oct 5:	Paul Thackaberry reports *Volcano*'s bow delaminating.
Oct 10:	Thackaberry out of propane gas.
Oct 12:	Minoru Saito taking antibiotics for toothache.
Oct 13:	John Biddlecombe on way to Recife for repairs.
Oct 17:	Biddlecombe announces he is retiring. David Adams reports broken gooseneck aboard *Innkeeper*.
Oct 23:	Alain Gautier first in Cape Town with *Generali Concorde*.
Oct 26:	Jane Weber on route for Barbados to retire from race.
Oct 30:	Five yachts finish within 10-hour span.
Nov 24:	*Grinaker* and *Duracell* in collision at Cape Town restart.
Dec 2:	Hal Roth heading for Cape Town with various damage problems.
Dec 3:	Nandor Fa heads for Port Elizabeth with two rudders missing.
Dec 4:	Jack Boye heading north with forestay problem.
Dec 7:	Paul Thackaberry reports broken boom.
Dec 10:	Paul Thackaberry at 56° 28″ south.
Dec 11:	John Martin reports autopilot problem.
Dec 12:	Josh Hall dislocates his knee in serious knockdown.
Dec 15:	Mike Plant reports losing all his spinnakers.
Dec 16:	Boye reports he has no halyards, no forestays, a broken spreader and is using only his headsail.
Dec 20:	Nandor Fa departs Port Elizabeth for Sydney.
Dec 21:	John Martin crosses Sydney finish line with *Allied Bank*.
Dec 22:	Hal Roth departs Cape Town for Sydney. Isabelle Autissier reports *Ecureuil Poitou-Charentes* has been dismasted.
Dec 23:	*Sponsor Wanted* and *New Spirit of Ipswich* suffer serious knockdowns in 60-knot winds.
Dec 24:	Seven yachts finish in 12 hours.

1991

Jan 14:	Robert Hooke's *Niihau 4* holed in collision with trawler and goes to Ulladulla for repairs.
Feb 5:	Hooke arrives Sydney for second leg time of 136 days,16 hrs, 40 mins, 42 secs.
Feb 7:	Hal Roth restarts.
Feb 8:	Philippe Jeantot reports bad knockdown; broken gooseneck and badly torn main. *Project City Kids* suffers broken gooseneck; Boye hit on head by boom. Jose de Ugarte reports many things broken on *BBV*. Kanga Birtles reports he's left his sea boots behind.
Feb 9:	*Servant IV* in collision with whale.
Feb 10:	*Volcano* goes to Bluff, New Zealand for fresh diesel. *Shutendohji* loses life raft. *Generali Concorde* hits 15.8 knots.
Feb 11:	Robert Hooke back at sea.
Feb 14:	Christophe Auguin reports visibility of 100 metres and icebergs.
Feb 15:	John Martin encounters 'five huge icebergs, and four growlers'.
Feb 16:	Nandor Fa reports nine icebergs. *Volcano* hits whale.
Feb 18:	John Martin reported that *Allied Bank* was last night in collision with a growler. Main stringer cracked in two places.
Feb 19:	Robert Hooke pulls out.
Feb 20:	*Allied Bank* abandoned: John Martin rescued by *Grinaker*.
Feb 21:	*Credit Agricole* in collision with growler, block of ice jammed between rudders for three hours.
Feb 22:	Fleet in depression registering 958 millibars.
Feb 27:	Alain Gautier rounds Cape Horn.
Mar 3:	*New Spirit of Ipswich* suffers broken boom. *Alba Regia*, *Servant IV*, *Credit Agricole IV*, *Ecureuil*, *Grinaker*, *BBV* and *Jarkan* all round Cape Horn.
Mar 6:	Gautier first in Punta del Este.
Mar 10:	'Magnificent Seven' finish in 11-hour span.
Mar 30:	*BBV* returns to Punta with damaged headsail.
April 22:	*Generali* suffers torn mainsail.
April 23:	Christophe Auguin first in Newport at 01:11:22 AM. *Generali Concorde* becalmed. Auguin is the winner.

The BOC Challenge results

Final Race Standings	Newport–Cape Town	Cape Town–Sydney	Sydney–Punta del Este	Punta del Este–Newport
Groupe Sceta	37-18-00-29(1)	27-00-45-02(2)	32-13-39-42(2)	23-14-11-22(1)
C. Auguin		64-18-45-31(2)	97-08-25-13(2)	1220-22-36-35(1)
G. Concorde	38-03-42-39(4)*	27-03-55-14(3)	31-03-21-14(1)	26-01-50-10(2)
A. Gautier		65-07-37-53(3)	96-10-59-07(1)	122-12-55-17(2)
Credit A. IV	37-21-11-45(3)	29-15-32-08(4)	35-10-31-11(10)	26-15-34-38(3)
P. Jeantot		67-12-43-53(4)	102-23-15-04(4)	129-14-49-42(3)
Duracell	39-11-41-40(5)	29-22-36-33(6)+	33-08-53-54(4)	30-00-48-55(5)
M. Plant		69-10-18-13(5)	102-19-12-07(3)	132-20-01-02(4)
Jarkan	39-16-05-32(6)	30-03-31-03(7)	35-07-27-48(9)	30-18-34-24(8)
K. Birtles		69-19-36-35(6)	105-03-04-23(5)	135-21-38-47(5)
Innkeeper	44-07-29-57(9)	29-16-18-52(5)	33-02-23-41(3)	29-02-29-50(4)
D. Adams		73-23-48-49(8)	107-02-12-30(6)	136-04-42-20(6)
Ecureuil	41-04-37-13(7)	32-15-50-31(11)	35-05-17-07(6)	30-03-03-40(6)
I. Autissier		73-20-27-44(7)	109-01-44-51(7)	139-04-48-31(7)
Grinaker	44-06-19-25(8)	30-08-34-47(9)	34-19-00-24(5)=	30-18-57-39(9)
B. Reed		74-14-54-12(9)	109-09-54-36(8)	140-04-52-15(8)
BBV Expo '92	44-15-32-13(11)	30-04-31-26(8)	35-06-07-42(7)	30-14-19-50(7)
J. Ugarte		74-20-03-39(10)	110-02-11-21(9)	140-16-31-11(9)
Servant IV	44-15-44-07(12)	30-12-02-13(10)	35-15-32-11(11)	30-20-30-56(10)
Y. Dupasquier		75-03-46-20(11)	110-19-18-31(10)	141-15-49-27(10)
Buttercup#	46-01-20-47(14)	34-16-07-31(13)	39-07-27-22(13)	33-11-25-40(12)
D McIntyre		80-17-28-18(12)	120-00-55-40(11)	153-12-21-20(11)
New Spirit	48-10-58-50(15)	33-13-52-44(12)	41-07-52-48(14)	33-19-23-55(13)
J. Hall		82-00-51-34(13)	123-08-44-22(12)	157-04-08-17(12)
Project	45-14-56-44(13)	38-14-35-18(14)	39-04-59-25(14)	35-05-22-32(14)
J. Boye		84-05-32-02(14)	123-10-31-27(13)	158-15-53-59(13)
Alba Regia	44-15-19-07(10)	53-00-00-26(19)	35-07-10-36(8)	33-00-55-38(11)
N. Fa		97-15-19-33(16)	132-22-30-09(14)	165-23-25-47(14)
Volcano	56-10-34-27(18)	39-06-49-20(15)	41-10-04-52(15)	43-04-11-04(18)
P. Thackaberry		95-17-23-47(15)	137-03-28-39(15)	180-07-39-42(15)
Global Exp.	57-09-40-44(19)	41-02-51-25(16)	43-07-55-26(16)	39-21-49-42(16)
R. Davie		98-12-32-09(17)	141-20-27-35(16)	181-18-17-17(16)
Shutendohji II	63-19-20-07(20)	43-13-04-53(17)	47-14-41-05(17)	42-21-04-54(17)
M. Saito		107-08-25-00(18)	154-23-06-05(17)	197-20-10-59(17)
Sebago	54-21-40-09(17)	67-08-53-37(20)	50-10-17-56(18)	39-00-21-01(15)>
H. Roth		122-06-33-46(20)	172-16-51-42(18)	211-17-12-43(18)
Koden VIII	50-22-45-16(16)	51-13-35-49(18)	Did not restart	
Y. Tada		102-12-21-05(19)		
Allied Bank<	37-19-47-44(2)	26-06-47-23(1)	Abandoned after hit 'growler'	
J. Martin		64-02-35-07(1)		
Niihau 4	64-01-37-44(21)	72-15-02-58(21)	Withdrew with gear problems	
R. Hooke		136-16-40-42(21)		
Kilcullen	Retired, following dismasting			
E. O'Coineen				
Interox Cru.	Retired, following structural problems			
J. Biddlecombe				
Tilley End.	Retired following damage and injuries			
J. Weber				
Zafu	Retired			
W. Gilmore				

> * includes 16.5 hour time penalty
> \+ Four hours deducted for collision
> \# *Buttercup* began as *Sponsor Wanted*
> < Rescued by Bertie Reed's *Grinaker*
> = Nine hour redress for Martin rescue
> \> 72 h 16 m 10 s deducted; late arrival rule

Glossary

ARGOS: satellite tracking system used to determine several times daily the precise position of a yacht.

Argos beacon: automatically transmits position, course, and speed of each boat.

auto-pilot: an electrically powered self-steering device that keeps the boat on a set course.

beat: to beat into the wind. To go into the weather.

boom: the spar to which the bottom edge, or foot, of the mainsail is fastened. The front end of the boom is attached to the mast.

chainplate: steel plate fastened to the hull or deck to which the lower ends of the mast's supporting wires are attached.

cockpit: the sunken area of the deck where one can sit down and steer the boat.

cutter: a single-masted boat with mainsail and more than one headsail.

draft: the depth of water the yacht draws from tip of keel to the waterline.

forestay: supporting wire that runs from near the top of the mast forward to the bow, where it is attached at deck level to the chainplate.

fractional: (rig) as opposed to a masthead rig, the forestay of which extends to the top of the mast. The forestay of a yacht with fractional rig extends only part of the way up.

furling gear: fitted so that a headsail can be rolled around the forestay.

Genoa: a sail hoisted on the forestay.

goose-neck: pivotal connection between mast and boom.

GPS: global-positioning system.

gybe: a manoeuvre where the boat's course is altered to bring the wind from one side of the boat to the other by swinging the stern through the eye of the wind.

halyard: the line that is secured to the top of the sail and is used to raise or lower it.

headsail: general term for a sail hoisted and flown forward of the mast.

headstay: alternative term for forestay: runs from high on the mast to the steamhead fitting.

jib: a sail hoisted on the forestay, slightly different in shape to a Genoa.

jury rig: a temporary but effective device which replaces lost or damaged gear. A jury mast may be made with the boom and spinnaker pole.

knot: a unit measure of a boat's speed; one knot equals one nautical mile per hour.

LOA: overall length.

mainsail: as the name implies, the main sail, hoisted on the aft side of the mast.

mainsheet: line that controls the mainsail.

181

nautical mile: equal to 1.15 statute miles, it is the mile used for navigation at sea.

off the wind: sailing downwind, or to leeward. A reach is off the wind.

pitchpole: the boat is turned stern over bow in high seas by a breaking, following sea that lifts the stern high and forces the bow down.

reef: that section of the mainsail that can be folded down and then tied along the boom – once the sail is partially lowered – to reduce the sail area as the wind increases in strength. There are generally a number of reefs on the sail, which are successively taken in as necessary. To let a reef out as the wind decreases in strength is to 'shake out a reef.'
router: a land-based provider of weather information to skippers.

satellite navigator (SAT-NAV): an electronic navigational aid that uses signals received from satellites to determine the boat's position.
self-steering: a general term for the auto-pilot or another mechanical self-steering device called the windvane.
sheet: a rope attached to the corner of a sail used to control the angle at which the sail is set. A jibsheet controls the jib, the mainsheet the mainsail, etc.
shroud: a wire that supports the mast, connected from the mast to a chainplate at the side of the hull.
single-sideband (SSB) radio: a standard type of ship-to-ship and ship-to-shore radio used for communicating by voice over distances of up to several thousand miles.
sloop: single-masted yacht with Bermudan rig.
spar: general term for all the poles etc. put on board whatever they may be made of.
spinnaker pole: a pole used as a temporary spar to hold out the bottom corner of the spinnaker, a large sail used when sailing downwind. When in use, one end of the pole clips onto the mast, the other end supports the sail.
spreaders: horizontal bars extending from either side of the mast, like crosstrees. The shrouds pass over the tips of the spreaders.
stanchion: vertical post that supports the lifelines or railing around the edge of the deck.
steering pedestal: upright pillar on which the steering wheel is mounted – it's placed centrally in the cockpit.

tacking: the moment the yacht is swung through the eye of the wind to the other diagonal.
to weather: the direction from which the wind is coming.
to windward: sailing upwind, or into the wind.
transom: the flat part of the hull at the very back of the boat.
trisail: a small, strongly made sail that is hoisted in place of the mainsail when the wind reaches storm force.

winch: machine for winding in sail lines.
windvane: a mechanical self-steering device, mounted on the transom, which automatically steers the boat, keeping the wind at a constant angle relative to the wind direction.
windward: towards the wind. To go to windward is to beat into the wind; to go to weather. The windward side of the boat is that side facing the direction from which the wind is blowing. If another boat or object is sighted 'to windward,' it can be seen by looking in the direction from which the wind is blowing. The opposite of leeward.

Index

References in *italic* indicate illustrations